# PAY IT FORWARD KIDS
## KIDS SMALL ACTS, BIG CHANGE

### Nancy Runstedler

Fitzhenry & Whiteside

Published in Canada by Fitzhenry & Whiteside,
195 Allstate Parkway, Markham, Ontario L3R 4T8

Published in the United States in 2013 by
Fitzhenry & Whiteside, 311 Washington Street,
Brighton, Massachusetts 02135

www.fitzhenry.ca      godwit@fitzhenry.ca

10 9 8 7 6 5 4 3 2 1

Library and Archives Canada Cataloguing in Publication
Pay it forward kids : small acts, big changes
ISBN 978-1-55455-301-3 (Hardcover)
Data available on file

Publisher Cataloging-in-Publication Data  (U.S.)
Pay it forward kids : small acts, big changes
ISBN 978-1-55455-301-3 (Hardcover)
Data available on file

Fitzhenry & Whiteside acknowledges with thanks the Canada
Council for the Arts, and the Ontario Arts Council for their
support of our publishing program. We acknowledge the
financial support of the Government of Canada through the
Canada Book Fund (CBF) for our publishing activities.

Cover and interior design by Tanya Montini
Cover image by michaeljung/Shutterstock.com
Printed in China by Sheck Wah Tong Printing Press Ltd.

In memory of my mother,
Margaret Evalyn Runstedler,
my very own Pay It Forward angel...
who was the first to teach me everything about kindness.

# ACKNOWLEDGEMENTS

Even the smallest act of kindness can send many ripples out, creating a chain reaction in which the end result is much bigger than it started. My tiny idea for this book, through the touch of many wonderful hands, hearts, and minds, has grown into something much larger and more beautiful than I ever could have hoped for. For that I am forever grateful to the following:

Christie Harkin, publisher and editor extraordinaire—you caught wind of this project when it was just a gleam in its mother's eye and you moved forward with the same passion for its subject and message, as if it were your own child. Solange Messier, uber-editor—for someone so relatively young in this business, I'm astounded at your skills and insight. I can't thank you enough for being beside me every step of the way, always ensuring this work would be the best it could possibly be. Huge shout-outs to my brilliant designer, Tanya Montini, my publicist, Cheryl Chen, and all the staff at Fitzhenry & Whiteside, a truly class-act publisher that I am so very fortunate to work with.

Charley Johnson and all the Pay It Forward people around the globe—I hope you will see in these kids a glimmer of yourselves. What you are doing in this world is so important and I pray you'll never stop. Humanity needs you to keep doing what you are doing. So many of you have become like family to me and I love you all dearly.

To the young men and women I've featured in this book along with your families—one of the greatest honours of my life will always be the fact that you entrusted me to be your voice to share your stories with the world. I'm deeply humbled, inspired, and forever changed by this experience and in meeting all of you. You have so much to be proud of.

For my friends both near and far, in both virtual and social media realities—your love and support continue to help me each and every day. My immediate family; my father, Edward, brothers Greg and Chris, and dearest daughter, Savannah—thank you for putting up with me during the very long hours of work in this project. Your acceptance of its importance to me was in itself a pay it forward. Know that it wasn't only me you were helping but hopefully many, many readers and those who could be potentially impacted by their very own acts of kindness, too. All my love.

"At last a book about the young change-makers in North America. They're nervy, brave and innovative. Their stories are inspiring and full of hope. These entrepreneurs are leading the way to a better tomorrow."

—Sally Armstrong, award-winning Canadian journalist, speaker, teacher, author and human rights activist

# TABLE OF CONTENTS

# FOREWORD BY CHARLEY JOHNSON

PRESIDENT OF THE PAY IT FORWARD FOUNDATION

The Pay It Forward Movement is simplicity in a complex world. It guides anyone who chooses to reclaim the human connection in an all-digital age. It is the one thing in this world that all 7 billion people can take part in. Whether you have money or not, you can wake up tomorrow and be a tiny bit nicer than you were the day before. You can make someone smile; you can hold a door open; you can do something for another human being that may just change his or her outlook. Pay It Forward encourages people to be a part of something that heals the world and makes it kinder for the future.

The Pay It Forward Movement is inspired by people who saw something they knew wasn't right and chose to do something about it, such as Martin Luther King Jr. and Gandhi. It is fueled by millions of people in over 120 countries. It becomes stronger every day by the people who choose to do something, however simple it may seem, to lighten the burden of people whose paths they cross.

Good people do good things every day, but we must not let the chain break. The act of asking someone to Pay It Forward is the quickest yet simplest way to make this world better. This movement removes all excuses; it strips us down to one human being seeing another human being and helping simply because help is needed.

The ultimate tragedy in today's world is not the noise of the evil but the silence of the good. The kids you will read about are far from silent. The world needs more action; the world needs more people to act on their feelings of wanting to do good deeds; the world needs more people of all ages to step up and do more.

The young boys and girls in this book are leading the way. They are just like you. They are your friends, your relatives, and your classmates. They form a unique group of kids who are helping create a better world—kids who will inspire others to do the same. They are showing us that we are all part of the bad that happens in this world, but we can also be part of the good, too—part of the solution.

# INTRODUCTION

The term "Pay It Forward" can be found throughout history dating as far back as ancient Greece. Benjamin Franklin used the phrase when referring to the loan of money. He suggested that creditors should ask their debtors to take the amount owing to them and, rather than paying it back to them, offer it to someone else in need. The creditor, then, is paying forward the monies owed to him onto someone who needs it more. He said, "This is a trick of mine for doing a deal of good with a little money." [1]

Many authors have used either the term itself, or similar words, throughout their works. In the novel *In the Garden of Delight*, Lily Hardy Hammond wrote, "You don't pay love back; you pay it forward." [2] It was Catherine Ryan Hyde, in her 1999 novel, *Pay It Forward*, followed up by the Warner Bros. film of the same name in 2000, that brought the concept back into the limelight.

## BENJAMIN FRANKLIN (1706-1790)

A well-known American inventor, statesman (someone skilled in government), printer, and librarian. He is perhaps most famous for his experiments with electricity and lightning.

A foundation was formed and the movement began. In 2011, however, a new person entered the scene and really shook things up. Charley Johnson, Founder of the Pay It Forward Experience, President of the Pay It Forward Foundation and Head of the Global Movement, left his manufacturing company, career, and millions of dollars in income to devote himself to spreading the message around the world and helping others.

Charley also developed the Pay It Forward bracelet. Unlike other silicone bracelets donned to support charities, these were designed to be worn as a reminder to do good, and then to be passed on to the recipient of your kind deed, entrusting them to go out and do the same. Over 2 million bracelets are now in circulation in 125 countries, without any marketing or advertising.

When I first came up with the idea to write this book, I thought that I might have trouble locating enough children to participate. To my delight, not only did I find enough kids to participate—I found I could have filled volumes with their stories. There were dozens, if not hundreds or thousands, of kids out there who never once stopped to think that the task ahead of them might prove too difficult—that they were too young, too inexperienced, or too poor to create change. They saw a need to help and they jumped in. While I am sincerely humbled and inspired by the fourteen stories I'm about to share, these experiences are truly only the tip of the iceberg.

In every case mentioned in this book, regardless of the difficulty of the deed or the number of times it was acted upon, the common denominator was that the chain was never broken. The acts of kindness formed a ripple effect and made an impact on the world. The kids you will read about in this collection come from all walks of life. They are of different ages, nationalities, and religions, and they live in different cities. They started their charitable activities for a variety of reasons. But they could be you. Paying it forward doesn't have to mean doing something big. It includes any act of kindness that makes the life of another person even a tiny bit better. You can start in your own home, neighbourhood, or school. You'll be amazed how good it feels.

I hope that this book will spark an idea in you and that you will be moved to take action. Perhaps your parents, teachers, and friends will decide to join you. I genuinely hope they will. And hope is a very powerful thing.

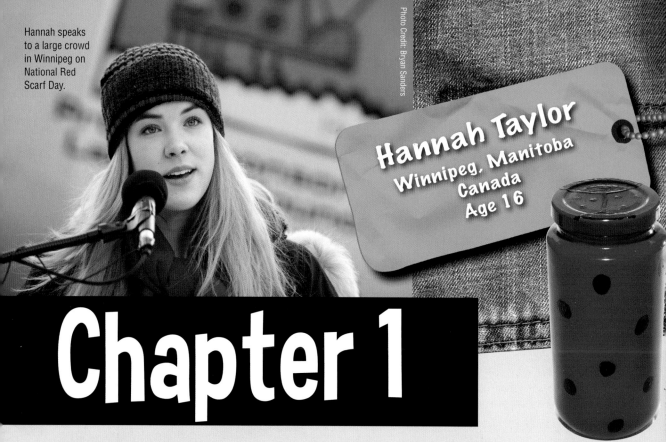

Hannah speaks to a large crowd in Winnipeg on National Red Scarf Day.

**Hannah Taylor**
Winnipeg, Manitoba
Canada
Age 16

In the hopes of bringing good luck, Hannah painted baby-food jars to resemble ladybugs.

# Chapter 1

# A Home in Her Heart for the Homeless

## IN THE BEGINNING

At the tender age of five, Hannah witnessed a man eating out of a garbage can on a cold winter day. Having no understanding of homelessness, she turned to her mother for answers. Saddened by what she learned, Hannah continued to worry and ask questions for about a year. "Why, why, why?" she asked. "If everyone shared what they had, could that cure homelessness?"[1] Finally her mother told her, "You know, Hannah, maybe if you do something about it your heart won't feel so sad."

Hannah understood that she was a very lucky girl: she had many advantages in her life that others didn't have. She was moved by a deep sense of gratitude—and it was this gratitude that made Hannah take action right away. She asked her first-grade teacher for help and spoke to her classmates. Together, they organized a bake sale and an art sale to raise money for a local homeless shelter in Winnipeg.

Hannah had heard that ladybugs brought good luck. She thought that homeless people needed luck more than anyone, so with the

8

help of friends and family, she painted over 1,000 baby-food jars with red and black paint to resemble the insects. They attached a small note to each jar, asking people to spare coins for the homeless. From there, things began to snowball.

## WHERE IT LED

By 2004, Hannah had established a registered charity called The Ladybug Foundation. She decided to speak out about the plight of the homeless. "My greatest hope," she says, "is that people see that kindness and caring can and will change the world. Walking past people suffering [...] will not make this world a better place."

Hannah has travelled from coast to coast across Canada, throughout the United States, to Singapore, and to Sweden, raising awareness about homelessness by talking to groups as small as 2 and as large as 16,000.

Hannah also loves to write. She used her talents to create an illustrated children's book entitled *Ruby's Hope*. In the story, a ladybug learns that by giving, she actually receives more in return. Hannah says, "I used to think if you gave things away, you would have less, but I learned that when you give from your heart you get so much more back."

Hannah founded a separate charity called The Ladybug Foundation Education Program.

///////////////////////////////////////////////

# Always try to be a little kinder than is necessary.

### —SIR JAMES MATTHEW BARRIE

\\\\\\\\\\\\\\\\\\\\\\\\\\\\\\\\\\\\\\\\\\\\\\

To raise funds, Hannah sells her picture book, *Ruby's Hope*, as well as red scarves for National Red Scarf Day.

Photo Credit: Bryan Sanders

## On Homelessness

As of 2008, the number of homeless people in Canada ranges anywhere from 150,000 to 300,000. It is a difficult thing to count accurately and there are different levels of homelessness.

Most people think "homeless" means living on the streets or in homeless shelters. But homelessness also includes those who live in vehicles, stay with friends or relatives, or in unfit or overcrowded conditions. Some people are temporarily homeless while others are permanently homeless.[2]

The charity's project, makeChange™, is a resource for teachers to use in classrooms from kindergarten to grade 12 to inspire young people and educate them about how they can make positive change in the world. As Hannah says, "Make change in the way we see the homeless, make change in the way we treat the homeless, and make change in the way we help people who are homeless."

On January 31st of each year in Winnipeg, Hannah runs an annual fundraiser called "Walk a Mile in Their Shoes on National Red Scarf Day," where she can be seen leading a crowd of people wearing bright red scarfs through frigid temperatures. To fundraise for

Hannah today.

her charity, Hannah sells these fleece scarves bearing The Ladybug Foundation Inc. logo. She also sells t-shirts, pencils, and bracelets.

Hannah also understood from a young age that when her dad went to work, he was the big boss. She knew that bosses had the power to make things happen. Hannah had an idea: To reach out to as many powerful bosses as she could, she decided to invite them all to lunch in large groups, rather than trying to speak with them one at a time. Hannah's Big Boss lunches are a way for her to speak with corporate groups to raise awareness and funds. The success of these lunches has been astounding—they have brought in approximately $1 million to the Ladybug Foundation.

Through her hard work and dedication, Hannah and her foundation have collected (directly and indirectly) over $2 million to date. This money has provided much-needed food and shelter to homeless people across Canada. It has also helped fund emergency and youth shelters, food banks, and soup kitchens. What Hannah really wants people to know about the homeless, though, is that we should "love them like family. They need that most of all."

## WHAT THE FUTURE HOLDS

While Hannah has had the privilege of meeting prime ministers, activists, rock stars, actors, and CEOs, she treasures the friends she has made while visiting homeless shelters most of all. One friend, in fact, has become almost like family. A former homeless person, Rick, or as she affectionately calls him, "Moosham," is now a member of The Ladybug Foundation's advisory board. In a sense, Rick is now paying it forward, too, by sharing his experiences in the hopes of helping other homeless people.

Hannah continues her studies and is hard at work on a new book. She has travelled to Sweden to be part of the World Children's Prize for the Rights of the Child as one of 15 jury experts. She also had the privilege of participating in Free The Children's We Day celebrations and speaking to thousands of students at this event. The Ladybug Education Program is turning its materials into online resources and hopes to reach even more classrooms.

### THE WORLD CHILDREN'S PRIZE

An award presented to 3 adult heroes each year who fight for the rights of children. Children worldwide send in their votes and choose the winners. Over 7 million students have participated in the program so far.[3]

Hannah wishes that her charities weren't needed and that everyone had a home, but until that day comes, she will keep helping those in need. Her motto is "Whether you are 5, 15, or 55, you can make a difference in our world for the better. You CAN do it. Never believe that a smaller number of digits on your birth cert-ificate makes you less powerful and capable."

Hannah feels lucky for the encouragement she has received and says, "One of the main reasons the Ladybug Foundation exists today is the fact that my parents never told me I couldn't do it." With a supportive family, an accepting group of friends, and a sky-is-the-limit attitude, Hannah still has many plans and many lives to touch. Though helping others is all she really set out to do, she also loves to see individuals that she has helped reaching out to others.

As to what keeps her going and inspired, Hannah claims it's the words of a small child who wrapped her arms around her at a homeless shelter and said, "Before today, I thought nobody loved me. Now I know you do."

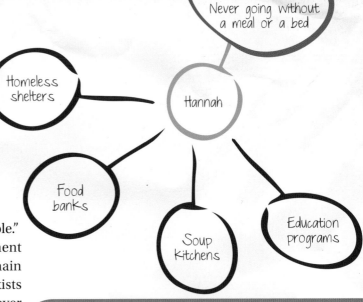

Never going without a meal or a bed

Homeless shelters

Hannah

Food banks

Soup Kitchens

Education programs

## We Day

Brothers Craig and Marc Kielburger—activists, humanitarians, and social entrepreneurs—began the We Day celebrations in order to bring thousands of youth together and inspire them, not only for the day, but in the years ahead. Celebrity speakers, entertainers, and social change-makers take the stage. Over 100,000 kids and teens have now attended events, with 5.4 million people watching through broadcasts.[4]

### FOOD BANK

A place that collects donated food and then gives it to people who are not able to afford to buy enough of their own.

### YOUTH SHELTER

A place that provides homeless youth with shelter (a place to stay) and, often, support programs.

Hannah and Rick walk together with the crowd on National Red Scarf Day.

Tyler and his friend with the four children rescued on their mission to Ghana, Africa, in 2012.

**Tyler Page**
Brentwood, California
United States
Age 15

# Chapter 2

# Kids Helping Kids around the Globe

## IN THE BEGINNING

Tyler's story began in grade four. At the age of nine, while watching an episode of *Oprah* on television with his mother, Tyler was shocked to learn about the plight of some children in Africa. They were being illegally sold into slavery for the price he once paid a friend for an extra bowl of chili. He learned that once the human traffickers buy the children, they sell them as slaves to new owners. In this case, the children were forced to work in dangerous fishing conditions. Children are cheap labour and their hands are small

enough to remove fish from tiny nets. They can also dive into areas of water that adults cannot reach, which can sometimes lead to disease or death. "They were fishing for twelve hours a day with only one meal and they have to dive really deep into really cold water," Tyler says.[1]

These children were just like him. He couldn't imagine living that kind of life. Tyler knew that he was fortunate to have been born into a family that didn't need to worry about basic necessities. He felt an instant spark. "For the first time in my life," he says, "I didn't need my mom to guide

## "Slavery" vs "Forced Labour"

Tyler explains, "Slavery is such an ugly word and I can't even tell you how many times people have come up to me and said it will be more comfortable if you use the word 'forced labour.' But I do not want you to be comfortable with this issue because the simple truth is, when kids from the ages of three to fifteen are being sold by their own parents for as little as $20—there's no comfort in that."[2]

me to do the right thing."[3] He knew he had to help these kids. Maybe if he helped them, not only would their own lives improve, but perhaps, in the future, they wouldn't be faced with the same tough decisions their parents had to make. Perhaps they could even help others, too.

Drawing from his love of food, Tyler asked his friends and classmates to give up some time on a Saturday to hold a bake sale, lemonade stand, and car wash. This initial fundraiser raised just over $1,100. Tyler had been told it would take $240 to save one child from slavery for a year. He now had enough to save 4.7 children. Tyler was proud of what he had done but wanted to know how much more he could do. Though he says he knew that "whatever the number was, it was never going to be enough to save every kid from enslavement."[4] After a generous donation, he had more than enough for the 5th child. Tyler set a new goal—to rescue more children by raising an additional $50,000.

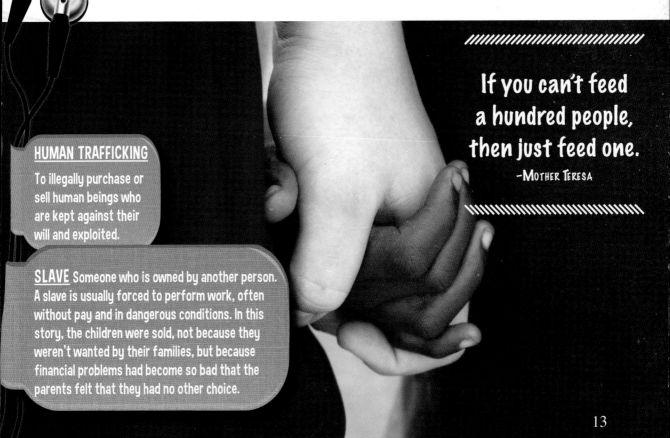

**HUMAN TRAFFICKING**

To illegally purchase or sell human beings who are kept against their will and exploited.

**SLAVE** Someone who is owned by another person. A slave is usually forced to perform work, often without pay and in dangerous conditions. In this story, the children were sold, not because they weren't wanted by their families, but because financial problems had become so bad that the parents felt that they had no other choice.

If you can't feed a hundred people, then just feed one.

—MOTHER TERESA

13

# WHERE IT LED

Tyler's desire to help others soon became contagious. After helping Tyler reach his first $50,000 goal, family and friends also pitched in to form the Kids Helping Kids Leadership Academy. This non-profit organization teaches children and young adults about selflessness, giving back, and self-confidence.

Tyler meets Never (left) and his brother, Welcome (right) who were featured on the *Oprah* television show that inspired Tyler to start his work. Tyler fed the 200 children of Never's village chicken and rice on their first emotional meeting.

Tyler helps Michael (the youngest of the 4 children rescued on his 2012 mission) with reading, writing, singing, and playing in the classroom.

Regular fundraisers are held for various projects, including a worldwide lemonade-stand challenge each summer. In the first year alone, $38,000 was raised; to date, over $200,000 has been donated to help children in Africa and across the United States.

Shayne Hanson of California needed special surgery for a congenital (present from birth) disease. Kids Helping Kids came to his aid by raising enough money to pay for the surgery. Four years later, Tyler says, "He paid it forward by donating 40 $5 bills ($200) for our rescue mission to Ghana, Africa."

In March 2012, Tyler, his mother, and a team of helpers travelled to Ghana, Africa, on a special rescue mission. The four children rescued on this specific trip were rehabilitated for three months. Then they went home to live with their families. They are now in school and get financial support so they will not be re-trafficked.

It meant the world to Tyler to meet the children he had been helping. Despite his nervousness, Tyler instantly formed deep friendships with the children on this trip. He gave out backpacks of supplies, provided meals, and purchased clothes for his new friends. The children had never attended school, so the group also spent time doing arts and crafts together, and teaching them the alphabet and how to spell their names. Although it was difficult to leave them behind and return to America, Tyler and his friends took comfort in knowing these children were now safe.

In return for rescuing over 100 children, Tyler and his fellow workers have received pictures and cards from some of the individuals they have helped live better lives in Ghana. Tyler says, "It feels really great that I'm helping kids from a different continent all the way across the world."[5]

# WHAT THE FUTURE HOLDS

Tyler plans to become an Air Force Academy pilot after finishing high school. He also has big plans to continue his work with Kids Helping Kids. He intends to return to Ghana every year to rescue more children and to build a centre of hope that would not only provide food, clothing, shelter, and medicine to the children, but also educate and inspire them to know that they can do anything they put their minds to. After five years of hard work, Tyler's well on his way to his ultimate goal of raising $1 million. Tyler also plans to expand Kids Helping Kids and create other leadership academies across the country. "The funny thing is, I've learned that it really isn't about the money at all," said Tyler. "It seems to me that it is really about connecting with the human spirit."[6]

Tyler has done some public speaking to raise awareness, including on the renowned TEDx stage, and plans to continue his talks to inspire other youth. In 2010, he was honoured as one of America's top ten youth volunteers. He finds the greatest reward in helping others to look at themselves differently—to know that they matter, and that they have hope for a brighter future. He says, "We as kids have a right to stand up and change what is wrong. We can do anything because we are the future."[7]

Child slaves in Africa

Personal freedom and comforts

Various charitable causes in the US

Tyler

Kids Helping Kids programs

## Human Trafficking - The Numbers

Worldwide, almost 20% of all trafficking victims are children. However, in some parts of Africa and the Mekong region, children are the majority (up to 100% in parts of West Africa).[8]

**TEDx** A world famous non-profit organization that was formed to bring people together to share ideas. Live talks are held around the world at various locations to promote learning, inspiration, and discussions about important issues. To watch Tyler's TEDx speech, visit http://www.youtube.com/watch?v=M82bntlVzc0.

Tyler with his close friend, Tette, who served as an interpreter on the 2012 mission, after having been rescued himself 7 years prior.

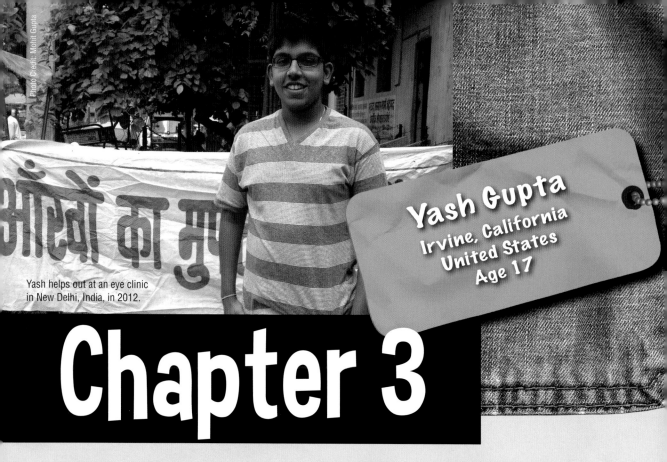

Photo Credit: Mohit Gupta

Yash helps out at an eye clinic in New Delhi, India, in 2012.

**Yash Gupta**
Irvine, California
United States
Age 17

# Chapter 3

# Giving the Gift of Sight

## IN THE BEGINNING

Yash has been wearing eyeglasses since the age of five. When Yash was in high school, his glasses broke, and he was forced to attend school without them. "Without my glasses," he said, "I couldn't see or learn in the classroom, and I was easily distracted. I was shocked. It was amazing how something I perceived as being so simple had such a profound impact on my life." Statistics show that close to 80% of information taught in schools is presented visually.[1]

> Eighty percent of all visual impairments can be avoided or cured.[2]

After a week of struggling to learn at school without his glasses, Yash finally received a new pair. He learned through this experience how difficult it was to learn without proper vision and knew he was lucky to be able to correct his own vision with eyeglasses.

Having done some research, Yash learned that there were millions of people around the world, many of them children, who were not getting a proper education because they couldn't afford to get glasses to see properly. Yet in his own country, used pairs were being thrown out by the thousands. Yash felt that all students had the right to own these necessary tools to succeed in school, and he wanted to help get these tools to disadvantaged youth.

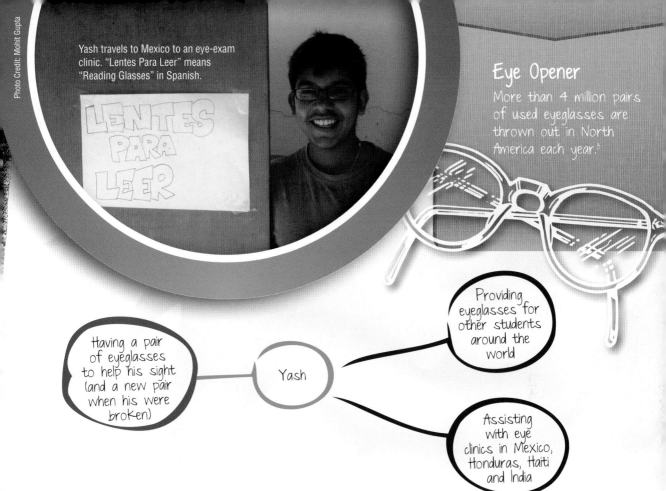

Yash travels to Mexico to an eye-exam clinic. "Lentes Para Leer" means "Reading Glasses" in Spanish.

LENTES PARA LEER

## Eye Opener

More than 4 million pairs of used eyeglasses are thrown out in North America each year.[5]

Having a pair of eyeglasses to help his sight (and a new pair when his were broken)

Yash

Providing eyeglasses for other students around the world

Assisting with eye clinics in Mexico, Honduras, Haiti and India

## WHERE IT LED

Yash started collecting gently used glasses. He received them from donors in person, through the mail, or in deposit boxes that he'd placed at local optometrist (eye doctor) offices. Patients at these offices would often donate their old pairs when they got new ones.

> "Kindness is a language which the deaf can hear and the blind can see."
>
> –Mark Twain

After a couple of months of hard work, Yash also launched his own website and non-profit organization called Sight Learning in January 2011. Since then, the organization has distributed more than $425,000 worth of eyeglasses, which works out to more than 8,500 pairs. Yash has also partnered with other organizations to run eye clinics. Some of these partners include New Eyes for the Needy, One Sight, Lions Club International, and Vision Spring, along with optometrists across America. Through these eye clinics, people with vision problems are matched to the proper prescription, and then given a used pair of glasses. For many of these people, it is the first pair they will ever own.

Yash with some of the children at the Mexico eye clinic.

## Access to Glasses

There are 670 million people around the world (10%) who are visually impaired because they do not have access to eyeglasses. Over 13 million children around the world need glasses. Many of these children risk missing their education because they can't see well enough to learn.[4]

## WHAT THE FUTURE HOLDS

Thousands of lives have been improved in Mexico, Honduras, Haiti, India, and locally in inner-city neighbourhoods in the United States. Yash loves to deliver the glasses himself and says, "The emotion on their face and their happiness upon finally being able to see perfectly for the first time is truly inspiring."

He believes that "seeing the impact that just one vision, one goal, can have, is truly eye-opening because it shows me that every person can make a difference. It is just about going out there and taking a chance and doing what you need to do in order to be heard, in order to make your mark."

Yash has been recognized with many awards including the Hasbro Community Action Hero, ABC 7 Eyewitness News Cool Kid, and the Presidential Volunteer Service Award, to name just a few on a long, growing list. His work is far from over, though. Yash's goal is to donate $1 million in eyeglasses by mid-2014. He plans to further his education and study business or economics before going to law school. Yash says he finds inspiration "through other young people making a difference, young people who follow their passion and use this passion as motivation to take action."

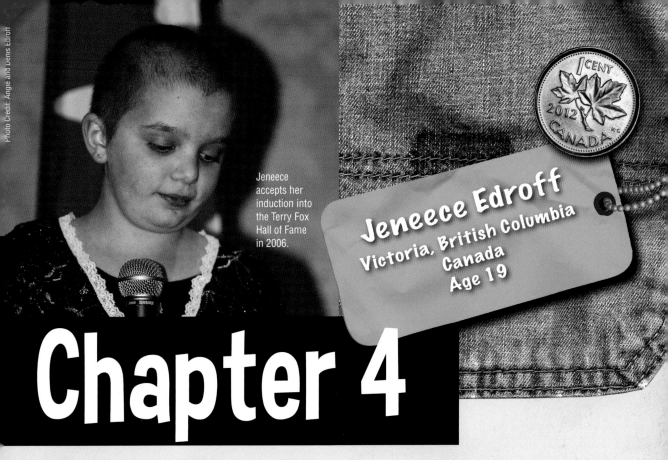

Jeneece accepts her induction into the Terry Fox Hall of Fame in 2006.

**Jeneece Edroff**
Victoria, British Columbia
Canada
Age 19

# Chapter 4

# Every Penny Counts

## IN THE BEGINNING

Jeneece has spent her life beating the odds. At the age of three, she was diagnosed with neurofibromatosis, a rare genetic disease that causes tumors to grow along nerves in the skin, brain, and other parts of the body. She has worn back braces, undergone multiple surgeries, and received chemotherapy drug treatments. She has been told she would never walk again or even live to be a teenager. She did not let this stop her. Instead, she decided to prove that nothing was impossible.

When Jeneece found out her family was receiving help from Variety, the Children's Charity, to pay for all her medical costs, Jeneece started collecting pennies to help pay it back, or in this case, also pay it forward. "This was an enormous burden on my family," she says, "I require frequent surgeries and medications that are very expensive." She knew she was lucky to have the support of an organization like Variety, and she wanted to help other kids and families with health-related challenges in the same way. On her first try, she raised $164 in pennies. Encouraged by her early results, she tried again and started asking for more help. The response was so good that she kept going. She soon became known as the "Penny Girl."

**NEUROFIBROMATOSIS** The name that covers three different disorders that all result in tumours growing in the tissues that surround the body's nerves. Jeneece suffers from neurofibromatosis type 1. The tumours have grown on her spine making her vertebrae very thin and unsupportive. This is can be extremely painful for her.[1]

"I am a bit like a penny, by myself," Jeneece says, "I am not worth much, but with a little help and lots of pennies, you can achieve a lot. Every penny counts and even the smallest person can make a difference." The coins continued to roll in and from the time Jeneece was seven until she was fourteen, she raised over $1 million. To date, this number has now reached an astonishing $8 million.

## WHERE IT LED

Jeneece continues to pay it forward on a large scale now, and in many different ways. In addition to her penny drives, which grew to become a province-wide fundraising initiative, Jeneece also participated in plant sales, auctions, hotdog sales, art sales, and many other events to help children's charities. Some of these charities have included Easter Seals, Camp Shawnigan, Tour de Rock, Cops for Cancer, BC Children's Hospital, and BC Neurofibromatosis Foundation. Other people, inspired by her work, have also joined in to help her or to start fundraisers of their own in her honour.

In 2009, Jeneece set her sights on another project. She wanted to build a place in her hometown where families could stay while patients received medical care at the local hospital. It would be a home away from home. Jeneece spent hundreds of hours working on this project. She partnered up with corporations, foundations, charities, service clubs, and individuals to raise an astonishing 95% of the $5.5 million needed in only fourteen months' time. With the help of 2,200 donations, ranging anywhere from a few dollars to one million dollars, she reached her final goal. In 2012, just in time for her 18th birthday, the 10,000-square-foot, ten-bedroom Jeneece Place opened its doors. It can now welcome up to 600 families per year.

Jeneece Place
A Caring Place for Families

Jeneece has received considerable awards and recognition for her work. In 2006, she was the youngest member to be inducted into the Terry Fox Hall of Fame, which recognizes "outstanding Canadians who have made extraordinary contributions to enriching the quality of life for people with physical disabilities."[2]

This young philanthropist had a big year in 2010. She started the year off as the City of Victoria's choice to be a torchbearer for the XXI Olympic Winter Games in Vancouver. She was also the youngest person in history to be awarded the Order of British Columbia, which is the province's highest award for those who work to help others. In May 2012, she received the Queen's Diamond Jubilee Medal, which honours significant contributions and achievements by Canadians. The same year, she was one of the final two runners in Rick Hansen's 25th Anniversary Relay. This event retraced the Canadian parts of the original Man In Motion World Tour, in which Hansen wheeled across the world for two years to raise money for spinal cord research. Twenty-five years and $250 million later, Hansen wanted to celebrate by participating with others who are making a difference in their communities.

One of Jeneece's biggest inspirations is TV host, actor, and comedian, Ellen DeGeneres. Jeneece says, "I think she and I are a lot alike. She loves to surprise people with money and cars and trips to make their lives easier. I love to do the same on a different scale. She uses the media to get her messages of support out, and so do I."

> # No one has ever become poor by giving.
> —ANNE FRANK

## WHAT THE FUTURE HOLDS

It has always been important to Jeneece to help and support other children with special needs in her home province. After finishing her schooling, she plans to take a year off, travel, and then tackle some more fundraising projects. "I want to help our local hospital with acquiring another isolation room for the paediatric oncology program." Jeneece also says she would like to expand the Jeneece Place idea to other locations in British Columbia.

Jeneece will also be participating in the BC Children's Radiothon for the 11th year, sharing

**PHILANTHROPIST**
A person who is active in giving and helping others.

**PAEDIATRIC ONCOLOGY**
The treatment of cancer in children.

Jeneece and Rick Hansen raise their hands in victory at the end of his 25th anniversary relay.

## Neurofibromatosis Type I

Roughly 13,000 Canadians are currently dealing with the challenges of Neurofibromatosis. Neurofibromatosis Type I in particular affects approximately 1 in 3,000-4,000 births.[4] No cure currently exists for this disease. Instead, treatment primarily focuses on managing symptoms.[5]

her story on air by spending the day answering phones and taking pledges. Money collected from this fundraiser is used to purchase specialty medical equipment and fund research to treat and find cures for childhood illnesses at BC Children's Hospital.

Though her health took a setback in late 2012 and early 2013, with the love and support of her family, friends, and community, nothing seems to stand in her way. In February 2013, Jeneece underwent her 16th operation to have a tumour removed from her leg. Despite some current problems with her kidneys, she has recovered from the surgery, is relieved from her leg pain, and has regained some of the movement she had lost before.

Jeneece's dream is to inspire and encourage others to get involved in their communities. "My friends know me as the girl who won't take 'No' for an answer," Jeneece says. "When someone pats you on the head and says, 'That's a big dream'—go for it. When someone says no to your request, just ask another person. Sooner or later, someone will help you."

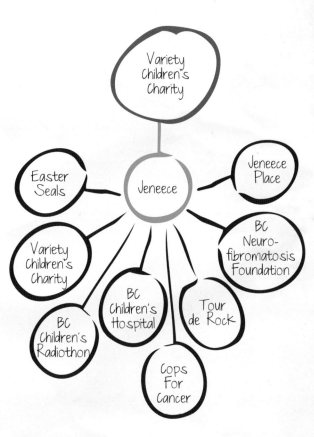

22

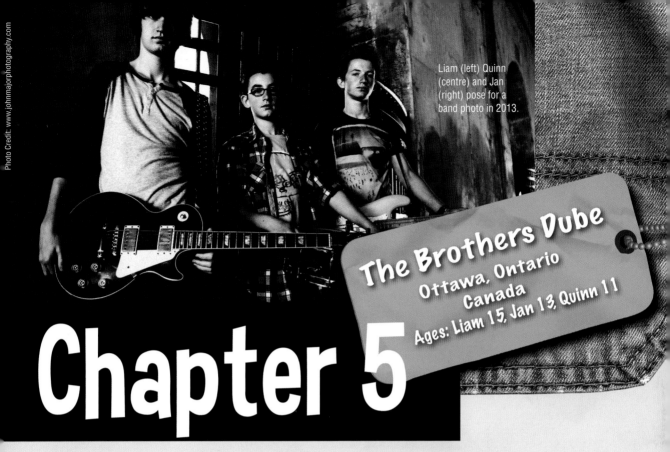

Liam (left) Quinn (centre) and Jan (right) pose for a band photo in 2013.

**The Brothers Dube**
Ottawa, Ontario
Canada
Ages: Liam 15, Jan 13, Quinn 11

# Chapter 5

# Hope and Healing through Rock 'N' Roll

## IN THE BEGINNING

Affectionately known as "Canada's youngest rock band," these three brothers—Liam, Jan, and Quinn—performed live over 100 times before they had all reached high school. Their musical aspirations originated when the boys were still in diapers. They would bang on pots and pans with spoons and play air-guitar on hockey sticks. After a few beginner music lessons from their father, they eventually took another six months of professional music lessons. It was their grandmother, though, who got the boys their first gig.

The turning point came in 2007. Their mother was battling cancer and the boys thought they would try to cheer her up by playing her favourite songs. They even posted videos to YouTube, and after their mother's death, they decided to raise money for cancer by busking in the streets. Then, their grandmother connected them with a fundraiser for a new cancer wing that was to be added to a children's hospital in Cairo, Egypt. This would be their first official fundraiser, but certainly not their last.

Liam giving guitar lessons to Haitian students. All of the instruments were donated.

**BUSKING**

To entertain or play music in the streets in order to raise monetary donations.

In 2010, an earthquake struck Haiti, leaving thousands of children homeless and orphaned. "We know how it feels to lose a parent," Liam says, "and especially for orphans that have lost both their parents—I don't know how I'd be able to live."[1] The boys decided to change their focus and start playing their music to raise money for a Haitian orphanage, a children's hospital, and other essential supplies needed in the country.

## WHERE IT LED

Soon the brothers began writing, performing, and recording their own songs. Along the way, word of the boys' talent and dedication began to spread, earning them several awards. One gig at a time, they got closer to their fundraising goals. At first, they only hoped to raise $8,000 but their efforts exceeded expectation; they've since collected well over $150,000. Quinn says, "When we first started playing in the street, people would just throw money at us...we would be up for hours counting it at home... well, we didn't keep it, we gave it to people who needed it and I'm proud of that."

By spring 2012, the boys visited Haiti. Every time the brothers delivered supplies that had been donated for the trip, they were met with gratitude. They also gave away musical instruments that had been donated and sometimes jammed with the children. After one of their performances, the brothers even left their personal equipment behind, including drums, guitars, microphones, and speakers.

While meeting with the Haitian citizens, the boys realized how truly lucky they were to have the things they did. The boys travelled through villages and farmland, to orphanages, and even to a new school that was being built. They wanted to understand not only the problems the people were facing, but also the solutions and plans being put into place. "We hope they might also find inspiration and hope in music," Liam says on behalf of their band.[2]

You can't live a perfect day without doing something for someone who will never be able to repay you.

—JOHN WOODEN

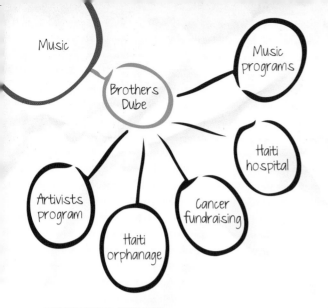

Music

Brothers Dube

Music programs

Haiti hospital

Cancer fundraising

Haiti orphanage

Artivists program

## WHAT THE FUTURE HOLDS

Life for the Dube boys has not slowed down since their return from Haiti. In addition to their concerts, performances, and ongoing fundraisers, they now travel to schools and provide workshops that combine a music set with a talk about their journey. Lead singer and middle brother Jan says, "Talent isn't just for show. It is a powerful tool for transformation." They call their bilingual program "Artivists

Can Shine"—a word play combining *artist* and *activist*, since they are using their musical talents to make a difference. The brothers want to spread awareness and invite other students to get involved. Their aim is to educate and empower their peers. "That's the world adults say they want us to live in someday, but we're the ones who have to make 'someday' today," Jan says.[3]

A second CD, merchandise, and an updated website are underway. It's no wonder that their fans, affectionately called "Dubers," are growing in number by the day. Even Canadian Prime Minister Stephen Harper wrote to the brothers to commend them for their work and to show his support. But throughout it all, the boys never forget their mother and what she taught them. She would be proud of the talent, maturity, and compassion her sons have shared with the world. Liam says, "Sometimes it's hard, but you just gotta get through certain things, and if you persist, it will be worth it in the end." As they say in the lyrics to their song "One," "We only get one life. Live it right...live it right."

Photo Credit: www.johnmajorphotography.com

### Haiti's Orphans

In 2007, even before the earthquake hit Haiti, UNICEF estimated over 380,000 children were orphaned in the country.[4]

Band photo shoot, 2013

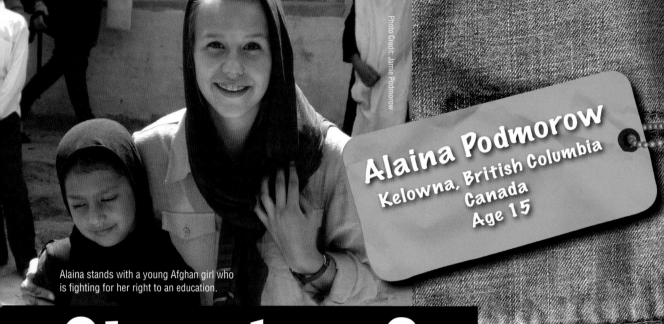

Alaina stands with a young Afghan girl who is fighting for her right to an education.

Alaina Podmorow
Kelowna, British Columbia
Canada
Age 15

# Chapter 6

## Because Every Girl Matters

### IN THE BEGINNING

Sally Armstrong—An award-winning Canadian journalist, speaker, teacher, author and human rights activist

In 2006, Alaina Podmorow attended a crowded presentation by author and human rights activist Sally Armstrong. Alaina would be changed forever by Sally's powerful words: "The worst thing you can do is nothing." Alaina was only nine years old when she accepted the invitation to attend the event with her mother, thinking at least she would get to stay up late that night. She had no idea she would be hearing about the human rights violations being inflicted upon the women and girls of Afghanistan. Alaina was horrified: "I learned that they couldn't leave the house without a male relative, could not get medical attention unless it was from a female doctor. But the thing that completely turned my stomach was learning that women and girls were forbidden to get an education."

These were everyday rights and freedoms in Canada that Alaina had never had to go without. Her family and her country had ensured that she would be able to go to school. Alaina made a promise to herself that she would do everything she could to help Afghan girls. She was grateful for her rights as a Canadian girl and wanted to pay it forward. Alaina founded a non-profit organization called Little Women for Little Women in Afghanistan. The foundation's slogan is "education = peace."

## WHERE IT LED

Alaina began by forming a team of eighteen girls from her local elementary school. They planned to fundraise and create awareness about girls' rights in Afghanistan. Other teams, or "littles" as they are affectionately called, have sprouted up across Canada and the United States. Initially, Alaina hoped to raise $750, which at the time would pay the salary of one teacher for a year in Afghanistan. She prepared a silent auction that was so successful, it paid the salary for four teachers! Some of the other fundraising activities that the girls carried out over the years include galas, bake sales, run/jump/bike-a-thons, movie nights, dances, garage sales, car washes, and bottle drives. Through funds raised at these events, combined with corporate and individual donations, Little Women for Little Women in Afghanistan has raised approximately $500,000.

All funds are sent to their partner organization, Canadian Women for Women in Afghanistan, where 100% of all funds are sent to Afghanistan. Teachers are hired and trained, rural libraries are created, and school supplies are purchased in an effort to support the education of Afghan girls. "Without an education, these females will not become successful global citizens and will fall silent," Alaina says, "[but] with that opportunity, these women and girls can become teachers, doctors, and whatever they dream of accomplishing."

Alaina has travelled throughout North America to create awareness through speeches, workshops, demonstrations, and media attention. She says that today's kids and teens are "the generation of change," and that it is "our responsibility to not only be aware of an issue in our world, but to stand up,

### SILENT AUCTION

A fundraising technique used by many charities in which donated items are displayed, then bid on by people attending the event. Usually the bids are written down, and the person who offers the most money receives the item, with the money going back to the charity or event organizer.

### HUMAN RIGHTS

Freedoms that should be guaranteed to all human beings, such as the freedom of speech and the freedom to work, regardless of who they are or where they live. A Universal Declaration of Human Rights was created in 1948, which lists thirty laws.

### BOTTLE DRIVE

Collecting bottles, usually soda or alcohol bottles, which are returned to a depot for refunds in order to get money for a charitable cause.

## Boys Versus Girls

The literacy rate for young women (in Afghanistan) aged 15-24 is 18%, compared to 50% for boys. Primary school completion rate for boys is 32%, versus 13% for girls.[4]

### TALIBAN ATTACKS

The Taliban is a military group of religious extremists who controlled most of Afghanistan in the late 1990s. It is known to be particularly violent and oppressive toward women.

### NATO COUNTRIES

The North Atlantic Treaty Organization (NATO) is an international group that was formed in 1949 to promote peace and security.

shout out, and take action." Alaina's work has been recognized through many awards, including the prestigious Me to We Award and the Diamond Jubilee Medal. She was also named the Top Teen Philanthropist for Canada.

Though Alaina had been pen pals with some of the girls she helped, it wasn't until 2012 that her dream of visiting Afghanistan became a reality. Finally, she was able to see first-hand the projects that she had helped to fund. She said, "We couldn't do the work we've done in Afghanistan had it not been for the help of NATO countries. They've made it safe enough for our team and our partners to run schools and other projects without Taliban attacks, they've swept for land mines, and they've built roads we use to access rural project sites."[1]

Upon her return from Afghanistan, Alaina said, "It was a life-changing experience. It was a great opportunity to see the projects we have been supporting for so long."[2] She's now more determined than ever to continue her work. "There were some eye-opening experiences that broke my heart and gave me more power inside and said this has to change."[3]

The first "little women" team marches for children's rights. Okanagan Valley, Canada 2007.

Opportunity to go to school in Canada

Education for girls in Afghanistan

Alaina

International Day of the Girl

Little Women For Little Women in Afghanistan

# WHAT THE FUTURE HOLDS

Once Alaina graduates from high school, she intends to study international human rights law. In the meantime, as an avid soccer and volleyball player, Alaina's next project is to implement physical education into the curriculum for the girls in Afghan schools.

Recently Alaina was appointed as a youth ambassador for Canada for the International Day of the Girl. This day, declared by the United Nations and celebrated in October, promotes equal treatment and opportunities for girls around the world. In that role, she was able to help raise awareness about the issues and challenges many girls face. She says that "if we are able to change the life of just one girl, we have done our job, and that is the most satisfying feeling you can ever experience." She is particularly proud to know that "somewhere in Afghanistan there is a girl reading or writing because of the work and commitment of Little Women for Little Women."

> **Remember there's no such thing as a small act of kindness. Every act creates a ripple with no logical end.**
> —Scott Adams

## Me To We Award

An award presented annually by the cofounders of Me To We, Craig and Marc Kielburger, as well as Canadian Living Magazine and AOL/Huffpost Impact, to ordinary Canadians doing extraordinary things to make the world a better place.

29

Noah Lamaide
Stevens Point, Wisconsin
United States
Age 13

# Chapter 7

## Dreams Can Come True

### IN THE BEGINNING

Noah Lamaide has never been a stranger to kindness. Raised in a home where the family motto was "teamwork," he had always witnessed the examples of his mother and grandmother's compassion for others: he says it "runs in the family."[1] The Lamaide family knew they were blessed and wanted to help the less fortunate. Noah's own charitable work began on his ninth birthday. He invited his entire class to celebrate his birthday by donating items to the local food pantry rather than bringing him presents. After the party, they were able to fill eight carts full of food, clothing, toys, and other necessities.

The first initiative was such a success that Noah decided to accept his mother's challenge and continue doing one community-service project each year. The following year, Noah raised $600 through a rummage sale and bake sale. With the money raised, he funded a picnic for war veterans. Not only did

**RUMMAGE SALE** Often used to raise money for charity, rummage sales offer miscellaneous second-hand items for purchase, much like a garage sale.

he purchase the food and arrange for live music, he even helped serve the meal and clean up after the event. This success felt so good that Noah created a separate fundraiser to help a girl visit Disney World in honour of her mother who passed away before they could make the trip together. In 2010, Noah also launched Noah's Dream Catcher Network, a website and blog created to spread the word and collect donations to help continue making wishes come true. Every Dream Catcher Network donor receives a small dream catcher key chain. It's Noah's way of saying thank you. With the Dream Catcher Network, Noah plans on "making a difference, one dream at a time."[2]

## WHERE IT LED

In January 2012, Noah encountered a cause that was much closer to his heart. He posted a message on his blog saying, "I want to help someone who is very dear to me for my next dream...My Grandma has fallen on hard times and is going to loose (sic) her home. My Grandma in case you don't know her has a heart of gold."[3] Due to increasing health problems, medical bills, and needed house repairs, Noah's grandmother was about to lose her home to bank foreclosure if she could not come up with $10,000 within just a few short weeks. Throughout Noah's entire life, he'd watched his grandmother foster hundreds of children in her home. "Sometimes," he says, "she gets kids dropped off in the middle of the night and she doesn't even know these kids."[4] They had nowhere else to go. The little white cottage had also housed three generations of his relatives.

Though the rest of the family had tried to hide the situation from Noah, knowing it

Noah collects new socks and underwear for needy kids in his community.

For his 9th birthday party, Noah collected items for charity instead of accepting gifts.

would upset him, he found out anyway and set about finding a solution. How could he not try, after all his grandmother had done for others? Having very little in his own piggy bank at the time, and with his own father recently out of work, Noah turned to the only place he could think of for help—the Internet. He figured if he could get four hundred people to donate twenty-five dollars each, his grandmother could have her home back by Valentine's Day. To everyone's surprise, people from all over the country rallied behind him to bring in $10,500. Even Noah claimed, "I didn't think I was going to make it. I'm grateful for all the people who donated."[5]

31

## The Dream Catcher

According to Native American-First Nations Ojibwe culture, the dream catcher is used to filter out bad dreams, while letting good dreams in. The good dreams slide through the small hoop in the centre of the dream catcher's web, and down its feathers to the person sleeping below it. The bad dreams, on the other hand, get stuck in the web and perish when the morning sun's rays strike them.[6]

Noah and his grandmother hold the Dream Catcher Network key chains.

Photo Credit: Jill Lamaide

> Do your little bit of good where you are; it's those little bits of good put together that overwhelm the world.
>
> —Desmond Tutu

For his next project, Noah decided to have a Random Acts of Kindness party. He asked friends, family, and members of the community to perform kind deeds for two hours then regroup to discuss their experiences. Each of the approximately sixty people who participated gave out cards asking the recipients of the deeds to pay it forward. He followed this up with a sock drive to collect new socks and underwear for the Fresh Clothes Project, an organization that helps less fortunate children return to school. On his thirteenth birthday, Noah collected hats and mittens for the Salvation Army. He finished the year by enlisting his friends' help for a gift-and-food drive, which they called Help Holiday Dreams Come True. Having already established himself as a young philanthropist, Noah used his reputation and contacts to spread the word further. "It makes me feel like there's more people than just me who think that everyone should get a present on Christmas," Noah says.[7] Through his experiences, Noah explains, "I learned that there are a lot more good people in the world than I expected."[8]

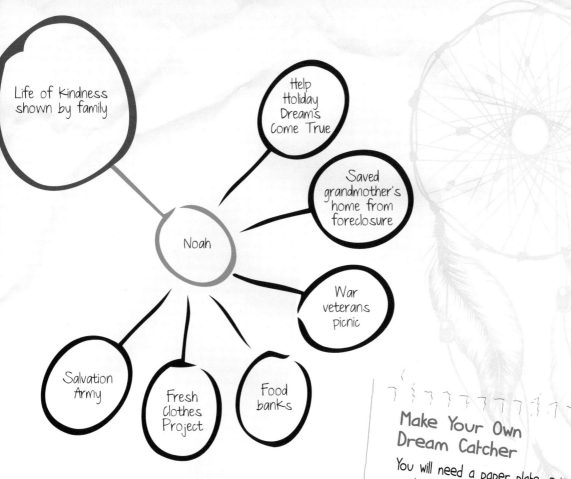

Life of Kindness shown by family

Help Holiday Dreams Come True

Saved grandmother's home from foreclosure

Noah

War veterans picnic

Salvation Army

Fresh Clothes Project

Food banks

## WHAT THE FUTURE HOLDS

Noah was overwhelmed with requests for help after saving his grandmother's home. He also made appearances on major news stations and had a segment run on the Disney Channel. Countless newspapers and magazines also reported the story. Noah agreed to go public because he says, "I hope my story will inspire other kids and communities to work together."[9]

Noah has no plans to stop giving any time soon and hopes to continue making dreams come true. His challenge to other youth is to "put away your video games for one day a month and help someone. You will be glad you did and it will make you feel good."[10]

## Make Your Own Dream Catcher

You will need a paper plate, scissors, paint, yarn, feathers, beads, and a hole punch.

Cut a large hole in the centre of the paper plate. Using the hole punch, punch holes around the inside edge. Paint and set to dry. Cut three long pieces of yarn and tie feathers to the end of each. Make a few knots to act as a stopper then add a variety of coloured beads above the feathers. Punch three more holes at the bottom of the paper plate and tie the feathered bead strings to these holes. Use extra yarn to weave crisscrossed lines through the holes at the inside edges of the paper plate. This is where the bad dreams get caught. One last piece of yarn can be attached at the top of the plate to hang it with.

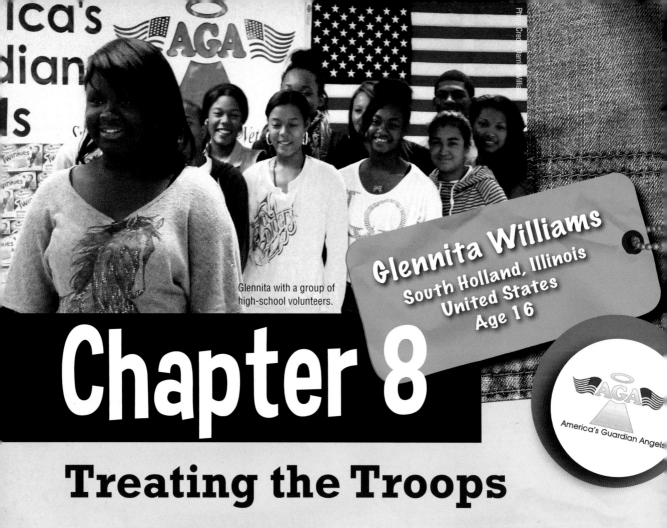

Glennita with a group of high-school volunteers.

Glennita Williams
South Holland, Illinois
United States
Age 16

America's Guardian Angels

# Chapter 8

## Treating the Troops

### IN THE BEGINNING

When Glennita was eleven years old, her friend's father was a soldier stationed in Iraq. His mission was to protect the Iraqi citizens from the war. Thinking he might be homesick, Glennita sent him an email to find out what he missed the most from home. It turned out that what he was missing most of all were Twinkies—the cream-filled treats. Glennita figured he probably wasn't the only soldier with a sweet tooth, so with the help of her classmates,

**VETERAN**

A soldier who has served in the Armed Forces.

she shipped out 1,000 Twinkies to Iraq. It was a small way to say thank you and pay it forward to those men and women who were risking their lives for her freedom.

### WHERE IT LED

Eventually, Glennita's entire community was committed to helping her cause. Businesses, churches, schools, and civic groups all jumped on board to donate what they could. Glennita collected, assembled, and gave out 160 care packages to a local veterans' hospital. This hospital visit would become a defining moment in Glennita's life. She says, "After every project or

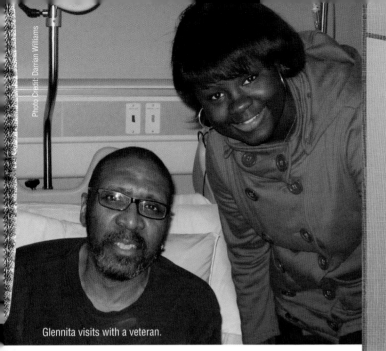

Glennita visits with a veteran.

## Dr. Martin Luther King Jr. Living the Dream Award

An award given out annually to people who strive to promote positive social change as defined by the life of the man that the award is named after. Dr. Martin Luther King Jr. was most known for his work in the African-American civil rights movement and his belief in equality and non-violence.

**As of 2012, there are over 22 million veterans living in the United States.[2]**

collection, I am always excited. I wish I could see the expression on the soldiers' faces when they receive the shipments. But when I see the veterans' faces, I feel that I have to do more."

So, Glennita created a non-profit organization called America's Guardian Angels, which provides care packages to past and present soldiers. She explains, "America is a great country...our safety and freedom has a valuable price that our troops and their family are paying. For this reason, America's Guardian Angels is determined to remember their courage and sacrifice." [1]

Glennita's packages include toothpaste and other personal care items, such as baby wipes (which the soldiers use to clean up when they do not have access to showers), foot powder, and feminine hygiene products. They also include books, handmade drawings and snacks, such as granola bars, sunflower seeds, hard candy, potato chips, and gum. Oftentimes, Glennita will receive wish lists of items from the soldiers, which she tries to fulfill as best she can. Sending the packages overseas is expensive, but Glennita and her

foundation have organized fundraisers and received donations to pay for the shipping costs. So far, over 2,000 service men and women worldwide have benefited from her efforts. Glennita loves to hear back from them and receive their letters.

## WHAT THE FUTURE HOLDS

Glennita has been honoured with over a dozen awards, including the prestigious Dr. Martin Luther King Jr. Living the Dream Award, the President's Volunteer Service Award, and Black Entertainment Television's Making A Difference Award. She was also featured in the 2012 World Almanac Book for Kids as the Volunteer All-Star. Glennita feels that her work is only beginning, though, and she has a long list of future plans. This honour student is a member of the Student Board of Education for her district, and President of her school's leadership council, in addition to being a Civil Air Patrol Cadet Sergeant, as part of the United States Air Force Auxiliary. She aspires to attend law school then become a US Senator, working with Veteran Affairs.

As for America's Guardian Angels, Glennita would like to start helping other first responders, like firefighters and police officers, who are hurt on duty. She also hopes to expand her organization to assist soldiers of other countries who are allies with the United States. Surrounded by loving and supportive family and friends, she is inspired by the courage and sacrifice of the troops as well as by others, especially teens who are out making a difference in the world. She says, "I have learned not to try and change the world all at once, but to do it one person at a time."[3]

### CIVIL AIR PATROL CADET SERGEANT

A program for young people ages 12-21 to be introduced to flight education, combined with physical fitness and leadership skills. Cadets can also earn scholarships to further their education.[4]

## Battle Injuries in the Iraq War

During the Iraq War, 4,475 US service members were killed and 32,220 were wounded. In Afghanistan, 2,165 have been killed and 18,230 wounded thus far.

As a result of battle injuries in the Iraq War, 991 service members received wounds that required amputations; 797 lost major limbs, such as legs. In Afghanistan, 724 soldiers have had to undergo amputations, with 696 losing a major limb.[5]

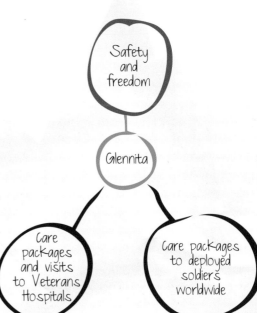

Safety and freedom

Glennita

Care packages and visits to Veterans Hospitals

Care packages to deployed soldiers worldwide

Darrian Williams

Photo Credit: Jenifer Pierce

Calista with her brother, Austin.

Calista Pierce
Guys Mills, Pennsylvania
United States
Age 13

# Chapter 9

## Caring with Crafts

### IN THE BEGINNING

Calista considers her big brother, Austin, to be her best friend. Austin, now sixteen, suffers from progressive muscular dystrophy, hip dysplasia, scoliosis, and speech and intellectual delays. His health worsens each year. Calista has always pledged to speak to him and about him or anyone else with special needs with respect—and she insists that all of her friends do the same. She understands how hurtful cruel words and bullying behaviour can be. "It can really hurt people's feelings," she says.

It seemed only natural for Calista to become involved both in the activities Austin was

**SCOLIOSIS**
A medical condition where the spine and back are curved rather than straight.

**MUSCULAR DYSTROPHY**
A disease that weakens muscles over time, often making walking difficult. Other areas of the body may also be affected, including the brain. The degrees of severity vary. There is no known cure.

able to participate in, as well as in the organizations that supported them. She loved seeing the happiness that Special Olympics brought to her brother and the other athletes. She cheered him on during bowling games (his favourite event) and

37

Austin and Calista get ready to go trick-or-treating for UNICEF.

## SPECIAL OLYMPICS

A worldwide organization where children and adults with physical and intellectual disabilities train and compete in sporting events.

was thrilled when he won awards. "I feel really good about volunteering every time I see the Special Olympic athletes excited when they find out that they get to go to a competition. They get really excited. They scream and cheer and some cry. It's an awesome moment to watch."

At the age of seven, when Calista found out that funding was running low and special events in their area may not be able to continue, she stepped up to help. She loved to make crafts and decided she would start selling them to raise money. With a little help from her parents, she started the non-profit charity Calista Cares. Her first endeavour to raise money brought in $27. Never discouraged, she tried again and increased that amount to $177 on her second effort. Her attempts to create positive change in her community continued to multiply.

# WHERE IT LED

Calista auctioned off homemade jewelry, seasonal gifts, and baked goods. She has volunteered over 3,800 hours to date, raising over $14,000 for the Special Olympics.

When Calista was nine, she learned about the Make-A-Wish Foundation. "It sounded like a great cause, so I decided to help by raising money to grant wishes. I really believe in the healing power of a wish." So Calista ramped up her fundraising efforts again. To date, she has granted four wishes. "My first wish was for a little girl who is four years old. Her wish was to go to Disney World," Calista says. "My second was for a boy who is fourteen years old. His wish was to see Taylor Swift in concert."[1] Another young girl also wanted to visit Disney World before facing her second open-heart surgery. The fourth wish is going to a nine-year-old boy whose dream is to visit Hawaii.

Calista has since added more causes to her work. She started her own team for the American Cancer Society Relay for Life and supports Trick-or-Treat for UNICEF. She has given up birthday presents in favour of donations, cut her hair for Locks of Love, and participated in other charitable events, such as Operation Christmas Child. Her generosity of spirit and enthusiasm have earned her a growing list of awards and recognition. She has already been featured in *Discovery Girls Magazine*; has won the local President's Volunteer Service award numerous times; has been honoured as the Crawford County Humanitarian of the Year for her work in helping others in Pennsylvania; and has travelled to Washington, DC for the Prudential Spirit of Community celebrations.

## Make-A-Wish Foundation

A non-profit organization that grants wishes for children with life-threatening medical conditions in order to bring them some joy.

The cost of an average wish in the United States through the Make-A-Wish Foundation is currently $7,500. Canada comes in higher at $10,000.[2]

Photo Credit: Jenifer Pierce

TOP: Calista designed the logo for her charity when she was 10.

RIGHT: Calista raises enough money to grant a 4th wish through the Make-A-Wish Foundation.

### OPERATION CHRISTMAS CHILD
A charity that distributes shoe boxes filled with gifts to underprivileged children around the world.

### PRUDENTIAL SPIRIT OF COMMUNITY AWARDS
The largest program in the United States that recognizes young people for volunteering in their communities. Awards are given to students in grades 5-12, on local, state, and national levels.

> Too often we underestimate the power of a touch, a smile, a kind word, a listening ear, an honest compliment, or the smallest act of caring, all of which have the potential to turn a life around.
>
> –Leo Buscaglia

## WHAT THE FUTURE HOLDS

Calista dreams of being an artist when she grows up. Someday she would like to be a head coach for the Special Olympics. She also has big plans ahead to continue her other charitable work. She is surrounded by friends and family who are inspired by what she does and encourage her to keep going. She believes that as long as you choose something that matters to you, "you are never too old or young, tall or small, to make a difference."[3] She continues, "It makes me feel amazing to know that I am changing the world and people's lives. I always get so proud when I reach a goal."

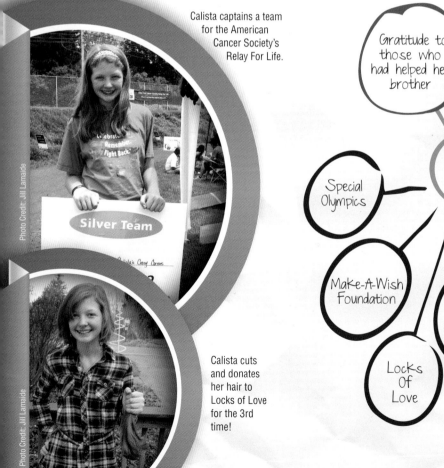

Photo Credit: Jill Lamaide

Calista captains a team for the American Cancer Society's Relay For Life.

Calista cuts and donates her hair to Locks of Love for the 3rd time!

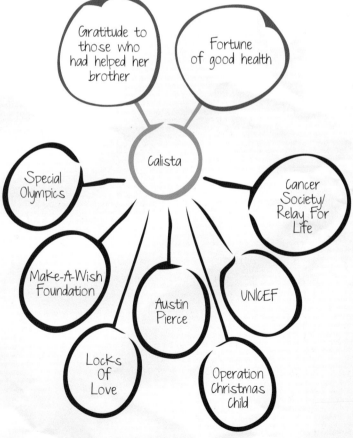

No act of kindness, no matter how small, is ever wasted.
—AESOP

Jonathan (Jack) O'Neil
Chicago, Illinois
United States
Age 10

# Chapter 10

# Even Little Hands Can Make a Big Difference

## IN THE BEGINNING

Jack was only six years old when he had to have surgery to try to correct a congenital deformity. During his stay at the hospital, he was comforted by a few stuffed bears that visitors brought for him to play with. These cuddly toys kept him company and made his time away from home a little more enjoyable. Jack noticed, however, that some of the other children didn't have any stuffed animals or toys to occupy them during the long, lonely hours. "When I got out of the hospital I was thinking about the other kids and that's when I started my charity,"[1] he said. Jack thought about the kindness that his loved ones had shown him when they gave him those stuffed bears, and about how much better those bears made him feel. Jack decided that he wanted other kids to have the same positive experience he had while recuperating in the hospital. That's when he formed Little Hands Make a Big Difference. The organization's motto is "the littlest hands can make the biggest prints on the hearts of those in need."

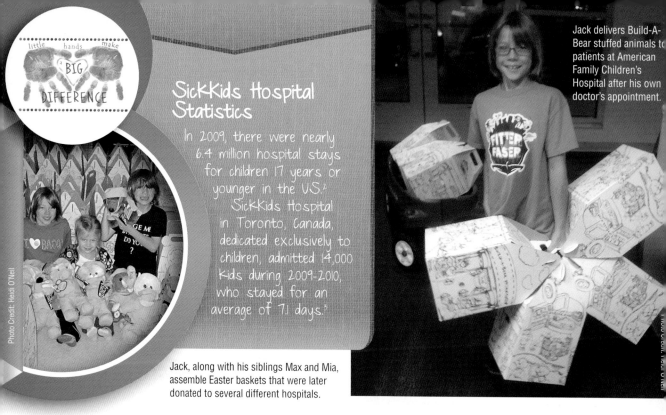

**little hands make a BIG DIFFERENCE**

## SickKids Hospital Statistics

In 2009, there were nearly 6.4 million hospital stays for children 17 years or younger in the U.S.[2] SickKids Hospital in Toronto, Canada, dedicated exclusively to children, admitted 14,000 kids during 2009-2010, who stayed for an average of 7.1 days.[3]

Jack, along with his siblings Max and Mia, assemble Easter baskets that were later donated to several different hospitals.

Jack delivers Build-A-Bear stuffed animals to patients at American Family Children's Hospital after his own doctor's appointment.

Jack told his mom that he wanted to raise money to buy stuffed bears for other children in the hospital. He started out small, as most kids do, with a lemonade stand and donations from friends and relatives. The funds started to add up so Jack began to set his sights higher. One summer, one of his lemonade stands made a whopping $800 in just two hours.

## WHERE IT LED

Originally, the bears Jack donated were dressed in scrubs like doctors. Jack had always been inspired by the staff in the hospitals because they worked hard not only to keep him healthy but also to keep him in good spirits. At Christmas, however, Jack delivered holiday bears and other toys and video games. He added Easter baskets and Valentine's Day treats, too. He also donates other toys, books, stickers, journals, movies, video games, and character Band-Aids. He wants to make sure the kids get to take his gifts home, so he makes his donations to the children, not the hospital. The bears soon featured every colour and style under the rainbow to match every special occasion. Whenever Jack raises enough money to place an order, he and his friends look forward to choosing which types of bears they will make for the children.

Over the last few years, Little Hands' fundraising efforts have grown to include an annual 5-kilometre run. With over 200 participants at their last race, Little Hands raised $10,000. That's enough money to donate bears to four hundred children. Jack claims this was his proudest moment to date.

Jack has been awarded the Presidential Youth Service Award. An initiative of the Corporation for National and Community Service (CNCS), this honour is given to residents of the United States who have inspired others to volunteer in their communities.

# WHAT THE FUTURE HOLDS

Jack has been inspired by many people on his journey. His family, friends, and those that have donated to his cause have cheered him on and motivated him to keep going. The doctors, hospital staff, and patients hold a special place in his heart, though. Jack says that when he grows up he wants "to work with hospitals and clinics that provide free medical care to kids that cannot afford to get the medical care they need." He also wants to be an Olympic swimmer. When asked how he feels about the charitable work he does, Jack says, "I didn't start this to get special attention. I give them [the bears] because of the way it makes me feel inside. I feel so good...like in my heart there are fireworks going off." Jack plans to continue fundraising and giving out bears and toys. He says everyone should "dream big and think with your heart."

To date, Jack has raised $35,000 and brightened the lives of 600 children in 5 different hospitals in his state.

Gifts from family/friends while in the hospital — Jack

Stuffed bears & toys to 600 kids in hospitals

My wife and I went to Children's Memorial Hospital yesterday to visit our son on his first holiday. His name is Clayton and he was born on March 23rd at only 25 weeks. It was a beautiful surprise to see a Build-a-Bear box under his incubator. We couldn't believe that he received a bunny on Easter, and dressed in scrubs. It was so cute. It was great to read a story about a child making such a big difference. We can't wait until Clay is big enough to help too...Thank you again very much for your generous gift. It may not have made Clay's Easter his most memorable yet, but it certainly did for his mom and I.

-Ross Carmody

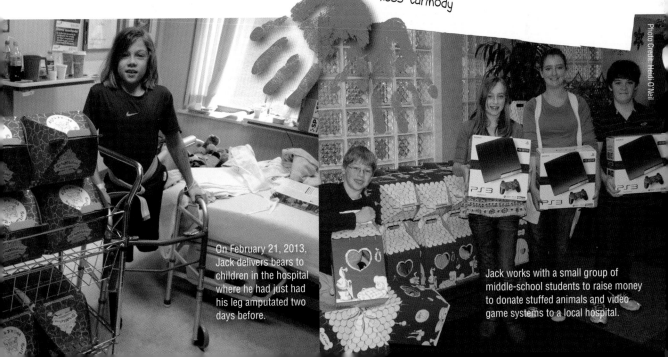

On February 21, 2013, Jack delivers bears to children in the hospital where he had just had his leg amputated two days before.

Jack works with a small group of middle-school students to raise money to donate stuffed animals and video game systems to a local hospital.

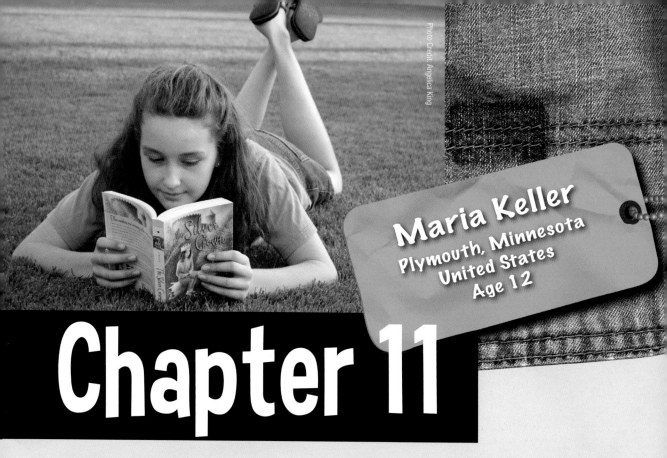

**Maria Keller**
Plymouth, Minnesota
United States
Age 12

# Chapter 11

# Making the World a Better Place, One Book at a Time

## IN THE BEGINNING

Maria loves to read. She's been reading for as long as she can remember. Her much-loved picks range from the picture book *The Giving Tree* to the Harry Potter and Narnia series among many others. Fortunate to be raised surrounded with books, Maria was shocked when her mother told her that many children didn't own a single book. Only eight years old at the time, Maria thought it was "kind of unfair that some kids got to have books and some kids didn't."[1] She loved falling into stories and getting lost in the adventures. She knew that reading helped her perform better in all of her subjects at school—she couldn't imagine never being read a bedtime story. Yet some children living in countries in South America and Africa have never experienced this pleasure. Maria also learned that people right in her own country, state, and city were also without books.

Having benefited so much from books in her own life, Maria wanted to do something to help other kids without books: "I wanted to

Children in an El Salvador orphanage are thrilled to receive books from Maria.

Photo Credit: Angelica King/

Photo Credit: Angelica King/

## READ INDEED

be able to give them the choice to be able to read."[2] She set a goal for herself: By the time she reached the age of eighteen, she would collect and distribute one million books to underprivileged children. She determined she would "make the world a better place, one book at a time."

## WHERE IT LED

What started out as teetering piles of books on her family's dining-room table quickly outgrew the space and moved to the garage, and then to a warehouse. There simply wasn't enough room for all the donated books in the house. Word spread rapidly about this young girl's mission. Book donations were coming in from all over the Midwest and around the world. Some of the books came from publishers and authors, but most were generously donated by the public through

**LITERACY**

The ability to read and write.

collection drives. At just eight years old, Maria recruited volunteers and soon formed the registered charity called Read Indeed. Boxes and boxes of books started to stack up. After sorting, categorizing, and packaging, Maria sent the books to children at schools, homeless shelters, food banks, orphanages, churches, hospitals, and non-profit organizations. She also sent out any adult book donations to new owners in places like prisons, nursing homes, and hospitals.

Local newspapers and a television station featured Maria's story, both to raise awareness about her cause and to congratulate her on her work. In the first three years alone, her organization gathered and distributed

////////////////////////////////////////////////

### Unless someone like you cares a whole awful lot, nothing is going to get better. It's not.

–Dr Seuss, *The Lorax*

\\\\\\\\\\\\\\\\\\\\\\\\\\\\\\\\\\\\\\\\\\\\\\\\\\\

45

# WHAT THE FUTURE HOLDS

over 600,000 books. Some books went to organizations in her own community, while others went as far away as Costa Rica and Peru. Shipping the books and paying for the warehouse space is very expensive. Maria has been fortunate to receive ongoing funding from individual donors and grants to cover these costs. She does try to match up international book drives with recipients in their areas to help keep these costs down whenever possible. "When I set that goal for when I was 18, I never thought I would be able to get halfway there in two years," she says.[3]

Maria has decided that she needs a new goal for her work: she is now aiming for 2 million books. At last check, her count was 805,748 books, so the first million is already in sight.

Maria is also interested in spreading awareness about the importance of reading and early literacy. Though she has been presented with awards for her philanthropy, what really makes Maria most proud is the reaction she gets when she tells the kids that the books are theirs to keep. "I just like seeing their faces," she says, "because they're just so thankful and happy."[4] She hopes that they will come to love books as much as she does. "I think they will be taken away with the book, too, and they will learn to love to read like I have."[5] Who knows? Perhaps they, too, will one day give another person a book to cherish.

Photo Credit: Angelica King

Photo Credit: Angelica King

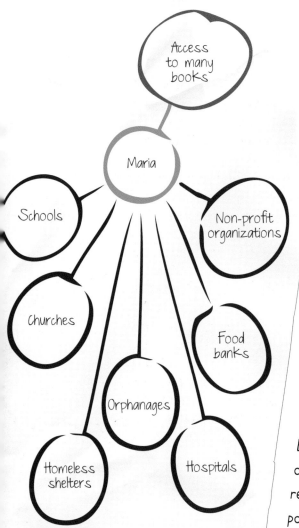

Access to many books

Maria

Schools

Non-profit organizations

Churches

Food banks

Orphanages

Homeless shelters

Hospitals

Finding the program Read Indeed has felt like hitting the jackpot for me. As a social worker, I am always trying to locate scarce but needed resources for our school community and especially students. Read Indeed is a goldmine because they allow me to put free books into the hands of children that otherwise would not be able to afford them; this is a first! When I tell students that the books are theirs to keep, their faces beam with excitement and enthusiasm, barely able to keep the covers closed. Some kids, who are used to borrowing from school or public libraries, even ask me twice if they can really bring the book home to keep forever...

I truly believe that every family with a child should have their own little library of books at home to encourage and inspire literacy. Having books around not only solves the issue of child boredom, but instills in children the importance of books and helps to create a lifelong love for reading. Our school serves a very disadvantaged population both socially and economically, so for many families the ability to purchase books for their children would be a luxury... We are so grateful to have benefited so much all because of one young girl's dreams and hopes to place books into the hands of every child...

Bo Vue, LGSW
School Social Worker
Hmong Academy, Minneapolis, MN

Photo Credit: Angelica Kilt...

47

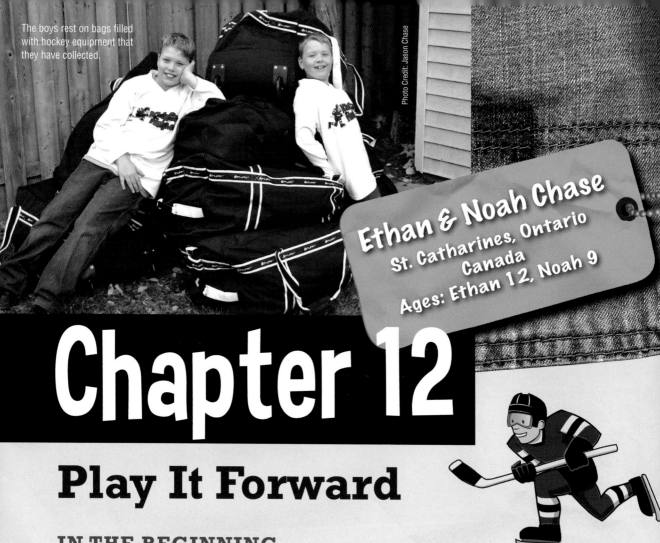

The boys rest on bags filled with hockey equipment that they have collected.

**Ethan & Noah Chase**
St. Catharines, Ontario
Canada
Ages: Ethan 12, Noah 9

# Chapter 12

## Play It Forward

### IN THE BEGINNING

Like many kids in North America, the Chase brothers love hockey. Ethan and Noah both started skating at the age of three and began playing hockey the following year. Saturday nights were dedicated to watching *Hockey Night in Canada*. One night in 2009, the boys listened to Don Cherry and Ron MacLean interview a player from the Bosnian National Hockey Team about the lack of equipment in his home country. "We thought kids in Bosnia could go to the store and buy hockey equipment," Ethan said. This wasn't the case, though. Unless equipment items were sent to the country, there were few opportunities for anyone to play sports.

Ethan and his friend Nick were inspired to share their passion for hockey. They started collecting new and gently used hockey equipment to donate to other children. Ethan's brother, Noah, then took over for Nick and started helping out. The brothers filled up two cube vans with hockey equipment, which they later shipped to Bosnia and Serbia. The vans were stuffed with over $20,000 of equipment that had been donated by friends, the boys' own hockey team, and local hockey associations throughout the Niagara Region.

Bosnia and Serbia

North America

Photo Credit: Jason Chase

A portion of the fees charged at this ATM go to help the boys with their fundraising efforts.

KidzCan Help.ca

## WHERE IT LED

After their generous international fundraiser, the boys realized that many families in their own community weren't able to afford the expensive sport, either. Their newly created website, Kidz Can Help, spread the word about their efforts and was a platform where the boys could sell fundraising merchandise, including skate guards, skate odour eliminators, mugs, lunch bags, water bottles, blade tape, and flask sets. The brothers began to form partnerships and accumulate items for local distribution, not only to hockey players but also to schools for skating programs. They held equipment drives, auctions, and fundraisers. Among their many projects, the boys were also able to send equipment to Ogoki Post in Northern Ontario and throughout the Niagara Region. Ethan and Noah have now collected over 1,000 pairs of skates, 2,000 hockey sticks, and an amazing $500,000 in equipment. They are grateful to their many donors and

supporters, including their parents who have always been there to help, driving them around to pick up donations.

The brothers soon realized that providing hockey sticks, skates, jerseys, and helmets wasn't enough; there were other costs involved, such as sign-up fees to play in leagues and money to pay for ice time. Due to these costs, many children were still excluded from playing the game they loved. With the help of their dad, the brothers contacted the Minor Hockey Foundation of Ontario, as well as local associations, to see what the response would be to offering the

### EQUIPMENT DRIVE
Collecting sports equipment, in this case hockey equipment, for charity.

# Nothing carries more potential for change than individual acts of human kindness.

—Jamie Winship, author

## Hockey Registration Decline

In Canada, the overall number of boys playing hockey between the tyke and midget age groups appears to have peaked at slightly more than 440,000 in 2009-2010. Since then, registrations have fallen two years in a row, dipping to 427,000 in 2011-12. Cost increases are one of the main reasons for the decline.[2]

one-day program called Let's Learn Hockey. This program is held in different locations across Ontario every year, though it had never been held in the Niagara area before. The participants would be selected by the Children's Aid Society and the Big Brothers and Sisters program. Once chosen, the kids would not only receive a full set of equipment to keep, but a day-long introductory training session. They would also be able to play a full season in the house league of their choice. The program sponsored approximately thirty-six boys and girls between the ages of seven and eleven. It continues to run in different cities throughout the province.

Ethan and Noah meet with Pen Financial, a company that organized the Skates for Kids program that sponsors ice time and provides enough skates for two schools each year. In 2012 the boys donated over 50 pairs of skates.

The boys also formed a partnership with Goodwill stores to run a Play It Forward campaign that helped to collect and redistribute used equipment to kids in need. And when people attended a Niagara Ice Dogs junior hockey game and used the Automatic Teller Machine (ATM) in the arena, Kidz Can Help would receive a portion of the fees charged to purchase more equipment.

## WHAT THE FUTURE HOLDS

By 2012, the boys were looking to expand their projects. Ethan suggested, "The equipment can also be used for ball hockey and we can get the word out to get more stuff with the ball hockey programs." The two brothers then committed themselves to help fund one child per year for ten years to play summer ball hockey. They also donated twenty sticks the first year. While the boys have met some hockey legends, including the "father of hockey," Walter Gretzky, the lessons they've learned about life have been much more valuable. Noah says that the best part about what they do is "seeing the faces of the kids we help and [knowing] how much fun they are going to have."

Both boys hope to become hockey-camp instructors in the future. They've also decided to expand their equipment collections to summer sports and have started collecting soccer balls and cleats, too. The first club to receive items for their spring 2013 season was in Concord, Ontario. The brothers also plan to send hockey equipment to neighbouring provinces in the future. Little did Ethan and Noah know when they put on their first pairs of skates that they would enjoy helping others so much. Lots of kids want to play. Some just need a helping hand. Both recipients of Peace Awards from the YMCA Niagara, Ethan says on behalf of himself and his brother, "We want to be good citizens and help everyone who needs it."[1]

Having the opportunity and financial means to play hockey

Funding for ball hockey programs

Ethan and Noah

Skates to local schools

Hockey equipment to kids in Bosnia, Serbia, Ogoki Post, Niagara Region

Soccer equipment to Concord, Ontario

Let's Learn Hockey program

**BIG BROTHERS AND SISTERS**
A Canadian volunteer program in which adults team up with kids to mentor them and foster positive examples.

## Jayme Morton
### Alpharetta, Georgia
### United States
### Age 12

# Chapter 13

中国

# New Clothes
# for a New Year

## IN THE BEGINNING

Jayme was only one year old when she was adopted by a United States couple from the Maoming orphanage in China. Although Jayme has always had a love of her culture and heritage—she takes Chinese language classes and attends a cultural camp in the summer—she says, "I don't feel any different from other children who have been biologically born into their families." She is just a typical middle schooler with a passion for horseback riding. Something a little unusual happened, however, when Jayme celebrated her seventh birthday.

She asked that her family and friends donate money rather than buy her presents. Her plan was to use this money to give back to the orphanage she had come from. She collected the generous offerings and then added it to funds raised after hosting a lemonade stand and emptying her piggy bank. She reached a total of $450. This was just enough for what she had in mind.

Approximately 100,000 children live in orphanages and children's facilities in China.[1]

## Love Without Boundaries Foundation

An American non-profit foundation that strives to improve the lives of orphaned and disadvantaged children in China. Their programs focus on education, foster care, specialized care for those with unique medical needs, surgical and medical assistance, nutrition, and orphanage assistance.

Children at the Maoming orphanage wear the new clothes that Jayme raised money to pay for, just in time for the New Year's tradition.

# WHERE IT LED

China has a tradition in which children receive new clothing to celebrate the Chinese New Year. Jayme enlisted the assistance of a charitable organization called Love Without Boundaries Foundation. Using the money Jayme had raised, the organization managed to ensure that all the children at the Maoming orphanage were dressed in new outfits in time for the holiday. This place had once cared for her and now she was caring for them in return. When she received a picture of the children donning their new clothes, she was so happy she was smiling from ear to ear.

In 2008, when Jayme was seven years old, she and her family made the trip back to China. Not only was this heritage trip a chance to experience Chinese traditions and customs firsthand, but Jayme's parents also took her back to the Maoming orphanage where they met the director in person. Jayme was curious about where she had come from. Madame Zhong, the orphanage's director, made special arrangements for Jayme's visit. Jayme's nanny, the woman who had been assigned to care for her when she was there as a baby, had the day off and went to visit as well. The director and nanny were grateful for all of Jayme's kindness in providing the New Years' clothes. They were thrilled to be able to see the young girl she had become since leaving the orphanage.

# WHAT THE FUTURE HOLDS

Jayme has since decided to forgo birthday presents every year and continue to raise money to donate to Chinese charities. "The last two years," she says, "I raised money for young children in hospitals in China."

Most of the time, you will find Jayme following her other passion, riding and competing on the back of a horse. "I would like to do something that includes horses when I grow up—having horses at a barn that helps kids." This seems like an attainable goal for the young girl who also says that "helping is something that will always be a part of me. It's one of my favourite things to do!"

Maoming orphanage & adoptive parents

Jayme

Charities for children in China

Clothes for children in Maoming orphanage

**CHINESE NEW YEAR** The longest and most important holiday in the Chinese calendar, Chinese New Year is celebrated for fifteen days. Customary celebrations include fireworks, family gatherings, special meals, and gifts of red envelopes with money inside them.

Carry out a random act of kindness, with no expectation of reward, safe in the knowledge that one day someone might do the same for you.

—DIANA, PRINCESS OF WALES

One day, Jayme hopes to combine her love of horses with her charitable acts.

Jack and Madi receive a shipment of official Pay It Forward bracelets. These will turn into lots of kind acts.

Jack and Madi Praver
Virginia Beach, Virginia
United States
Ages: Jack 13, Madi 16

# Chapter 14

# Fighting Bullying with Kindness

## IN THE BEGINNING

From as early as five years old, Jack remembers wishing for peace. As a young child, he found himself on the receiving end of teasing and taunting. His initial reaction was anger, but he soon realized that following the bully's example was not the solution. He decided to fight back with kindness instead and made arrangements to speak with his school to see if there was something he could do to improve the situation. Though he was able to move past the bullying, he wanted to ensure that other kids who were bullied at

his school could turn to someone for help. In the beginning of grade five, Jack says, "I went back to school with a plan, an idea to change the world...at least my world." While the school administration loved his ideas, for one reason or another, his attempts were delayed. He decided to take matters into his own hands and turned to his older sister, Madi, for help.

Jack and Madi's goal was to form a program that would inspire other kids to be kind and thoughtful, thus eliminating hate

and bullying while making the world a kinder place. A poster in their home from the Warner Bros. movie *Pay It Forward,* in which a young boy tries to change the world through kind acts that are "paid forward" rather than back, gave them the inspiration for the name of their organization, Pay It Forward Kids. Jack and Madi's mission is to change the world, one good deed at a time—"For Kids by Kids...Pay It Forward Kids."

In 2011, the siblings had the chance to hear Charley Johnson, president of the official Pay It Forward Foundation, speak at a nearby school. Johnson loved what the kids were working on. It was a perfect match leading to a partnership with the Global Movement. Later that year, armed with one hundred Pay It Forward bracelets, the kids took part in an Acts of Kindness European Tour. With the help of their family, the bracelets had all been distributed in eleven days. Even where recipients did not speak the same language, the message of Pay It Forward was still clear and appreciated. Now, Jack and Madi have their own Pay It Forward Kids bracelets to share with the world.

"It's about doing good stuff for others and then you expect nothing in return," Jack says.[1]

## WHERE IT LED

Jack's first mission was to start Kind Campaigns in elementary schools, challenging students to adopt a generous attitude and perform random acts of kindness. Through the use of personalized videos and Skype calls, Jack and Madi connect with the groups to deliver

## There is no such thing as can't.

—CHRISTOPHER REEVE

their message. The school then holds an assembly afterwards where each student is given a bracelet. When the children perform their good deeds, they remove the bracelet from their wrists and give it to the receivers, asking them to go out and pay it forward, too. The California Department of Education recently presented the siblings with an honorary service award for their work with a school in California.

The kids organize Giving Campaigns at different times throughout the year. Jack will choose individuals and organizations to donate time or items to, and then round up a

ABOVE: PIF Kids go bowling with friends with special needs.

RIGHT: Jack goes shopping to help a young boy whose family lost their possessions in a fire.

Photo Credit: Whitney Elliott

The official Pay It Forward bracelets have been sent to over 2 million people in 125 countries.[2]

crew of volunteers to help him, Madi included. With donations from companies, friends, family, and other compassionate people, Pay It Forward Kids was able to help over one hundred homeless children receive presents at Christmas. They've donated knitted caps to a cancer ward at a children's hospital, made cookies for the sick, delivered meals at Thanksgiving, skated and bowled with children suffering from debilitating diseases, collected shoes for children in Nevada, and put together care kits for the victims of Hurricane Sandy. Jack says, "I love making people smile. Especially kids that are younger than me."

## WHAT THE FUTURE HOLDS

Jack's latest endeavour is what he calls a "drive-by." He arrives at a friend's house unannounced and shouts, "Are you ready? It's time for a drive-by!" Then, they set out to perform random acts of kindness together while wearing Pay It Forward Kids shirts and bracelets. Most of the acts are very simple and often do not cost much, or even any, money. They will hold doors open, put shopping carts away at the grocery store, provide a cool drink to a lifeguard on a hot day, leave change at a vending machine so the next person's selection is free, or pay for the order behind them in a drive-thru restaurant. Jack says, "Every kind act that I

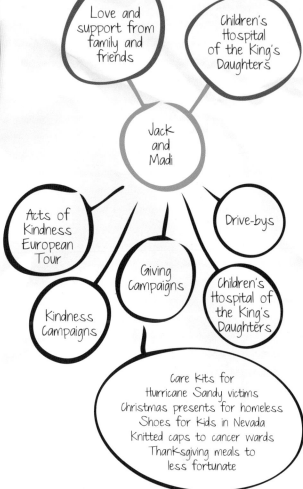

do makes me feel awesome. But it's when one of my friends looks at me, as many of them have, and says 'Let's do a drive-by and make someone's day'...that's the best."

Though Jack has had lots of people offer him money for his cause, he has chosen to wait until his government application for non-profit status is approved before collecting any funds this way. In the meantime, he gladly accepts donations of items, which he then gives away in his Giving Campaigns. The little monetary acts that he performs are currently being funded by his family and his parents' friends, but it is the acts of kindness that don't cost any money that are his favourites.

Jack also began his own vending machine business. The profits he makes were originally donated to The Children's Hospital of the King's Daughters in Virginia, where doctors saved Madi's life after she suffered from a bacterial infection when she was four years old. Now the profits go to help fund Pay It Forward Kids.

Jack explains, "...I want to be that kid that makes the other kids want to be nice...Just wait 'til you see what I am going to do." In March 2013, Jack was presented with the Helen P. Shropshire Human Rights Youth Award by the Virginia Beach Human Rights Commission. Winning recipients are selected based on their activism with social awareness, cultural diversity, and human rights in the community.

The *Pay It Forward* movie, starring Haley Joel Osment, was based on the book of the same title by Catherine Ryan Hyde, which actually came out first.[3]

# GET STARTED!

Even after reading the stories you've just read, you may still be wondering what one kid can do to make a difference. You may think that a small act of kindness isn't going to change the world...but it can! Anything you do to improve the life of another human being, to make his or her day just a little bit better, is progress. In turn, that person may pay it forward for someone else, who does it for someone else, and so on, creating a ripple effect beyond what can be calculated. How can we solve any of the world's bigger problems, if at the core of humanity, we do not truly care about one another?

Don't know where to start? Think about what you appreciate having in your own life: family, friends, teachers, coaches; opportunities to learn and grow; food, shelter, and clean water. Look around your home, your classroom, or your playground. There are opportunities to pay it forward all around you every day.

Hold open a door, give someone a hug, share your lunch, rake leaves for a senior, read to a toddler, give out genuine compliments, or walk your neighbour's dog. The list is endless. The Internet is also full of ideas to get you started. Pass on your Pay It Forward bracelet when you're done, if you have one, and then request that the person you gave it to keep the kindness going. Being kind is cool and you'll be surprised how contagious it is.

Kindness doesn't have to come with a cost and there are no boundaries. Anyone, anywhere in the world, can become involved in this Movement. Your actions could completely turn a person's life around. Margaret Mead once said, "Never doubt that a small group of thoughtful, committed citizens can change the world. Indeed, it is the only thing that ever has." So what are you waiting for? Get started. Remember to ask yourself each and every day—what can I do to pay it forward today?

# FURTHER READING

To contact any organization featured in this book, visit www.fitzhenry.ca/payitforwardkids

Clark, Sondra. *77 Creative Ways Kids Can Serve.* Indianapolis, IN: Wesleyan Pub. House, 2008. Print.

Cuyler, Margery, and Sachiko Yoshikawa. *Kindness Is Cooler, Mrs. Ruler.* New York: Simon & Schuster for Young Readers, 2007. Print.

Hyde, Catherine Ryan. *Pay It Forward: A Novel.* New York: Simon & Schuster, 1999. Print.

Lee, Spike, Tonya Lewis. Lee, and Sean Qualls. *Giant Steps to Change the World.* New York: Simon & Schuster for Young Readers, 2011. Print.

Lewis, Barbara A. *The Teen Guide to Global Action: How to Connect with Others (Near & Far) to Create Social Change.* Minneapolis: Free Spirit Pub., 2008. Print.

Lublin, Nancy, Vanessa Martir, and Julia Steers. *Do Something!: A Handbook for Young Activists.* New York: Workman Pub., 2010. Print.

Milway, Katie Smith, and Eugenie Fernandes. *One Hen: How One Small Loan Made a Big Difference.* Toronto: Kids Can Press, 2008. Print.

Pearson, Emily, and Fumi Kosaka. *Ordinary Mary's Extraordinary Deed.* Layton, UT: Gibbs Smith, 2002. Print.

Shoveller, Herb. *Ryan and Jimmy: And the Well in Africa That Brought Them Together.* Toronto: Kids Can Press, 2006. Print.

Walters, Eric. *Tell Me Why: How Young People Can Change the World.* Toronto: Doubleday Canada, 2008. Print.

Wilson, Janet. *One Peace: True Stories of Young Activists.* Victoria, BC: Orca Book Publishers, 2008. Print.

Zeiler, Freddi. *A Kid's Guide to Giving: By Kids for Kids.* Norwalk, CT: InnovativeKids, 2006. Print.

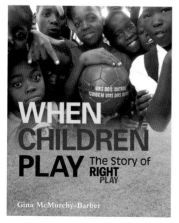

# ENDNOTES

**INTRODUCTION**

1.   "Franklin to Benjamin Webb (1784)." Wikisource. N.p., n.d. Web. 03 June 2013. <http://en.wikisource.org/wiki/Franklin_to_Benjamin_Webb>.

2.   Hammond, Lily Hardy. *In the Garden of Delight* (New York: Thomas Y. Crowell, 1916.), 209.

**CHAPTER 1**

1.   "Dumpster"" Ladybug Foundation. Web. 02 Feb. 2013. <http://www.ladybugfoundation.ca/>.

2.   Echenberg, Havi, and Hilary Jensen. "Current Publications: Social Affairs and Population.": Defining and Enumerating Homelessness in Canada (PRB 08-30E). N.p., n.d. 29 Dec. 2008. Web. 03 May 2013.

3.   World's Children's Prize. N.p., n.d. Web. 29 May 2013. <http://worldschildrensprize.org/>.

4.   "The Movement of Our Time." We Day. N.p., n.d. Web. 29 May 2013. <http://www.weday.com/marc-and-craig/the-movement-of-our-time/>.

**CHAPTER 2**

1.   "Kids Helping Kids." YouTube. YouTube, 11 Oct. 2007. Web. 02 Feb. 2013. <http://www.youtube.com/watch?v=Dpa9Z7NFUZo>.

2.   "TEDxRedmond - Tyler Page - Kids Helping Kids." YouTube. YouTube, 04 Jan. 2012. Web. 02 Feb. 2013. <http://www.youtube.com/watch?v=M82bntIVzc0>.

3.   TEDxRedmond - Tyler Page - Kids Helping Kids." YouTube. YouTube, 04 Jan. 2012. Web. 02 Feb. 2013. <http://www.youtube.com/watch?v=M82bntIVzc0>.

4.   TEDxRedmond - Tyler Page - Kids Helping Kids." YouTube. YouTube, 04 Jan. 2012. Web. 02 Feb. 2013. <http://www.youtube.com/watch?v=M82bntIVzc0>.

5.   Kids Helping Kids." YouTube. YouTube, 11 Oct. 2007. Web. 02 Feb. 2013. <http://www.youtube.com/watch?v=Dpa9Z7NFUZo>.

6.   "California's Tyler Page of Brentwood Named One of America's Top Ten Youth Volunteers." California's Tyler Page of Brentwood Named One of America's Top Ten Youth Volunteers. 2 May 2011. Web. 02 Feb. 2013. <http://www.businesswire.com/news/home/20110502006639/en/California's-Tyler-Page-Brentwood-Named-America's-Top>.

7.   "TEDxRedmond - Tyler Page - Kids Helping Kids." YouTube. YouTube, 04 Jan. 2012. Web. 02 Feb. 2013. <http://www.youtube.com/watch?v=M82bntIVzc0>.

8.   Richards, Martha. "Human Trafficking." AfricaStories RSS. N.p., 08 Apr. 2010. Web. 03 May 2013.

**CHAPTER 3**

1.   "MSN Kid Wonder." Sight Learning - News/Media. N.p., n.d. Web. 03 June 2013.

2.   "Visual Impairment and Blindness." World Health Organization. N.p., n.d. Web. 05 June 2013. http://www.who.int/mediacentre/factsheets/fs282/en/.

3.   "Vision For The World." EYEsee. N.p., n.d. Web. 04 June 2013. http://eyeseemission.org/

4.   "Key Facts." Vision Aid Overseas. N.p., n.d. Web. 27 May 2013. <http://www.visionaidoverseas.org/key-facts>.

**CHAPTER 4**

1.   "Neurofibromatosis." MediResource's Body and Health. N.p., n.d. Web. 03 May 2013.

2.   "Canadian Foundation for Physically Disabled Persons." Canadian Foundation for Physically Disabled Persons. Web. 02 Feb. 2013. <http://www3.sympatico.ca/whynot/events/halloffame.html>.

3. Together, Inspiring Hope, Enriching Lives, and Building a Better Future for Children in BC Who Have Special Needs." Variety - The Children's Charity of British Columbia. N.p., n.d. Web. 29 May 2013. http://www.variety.bc.ca/.

4. "NF1." The British Columbia Neurofibromatosis Foundation (BCNF). N.p., n.d. Web. 03 May 2013. http://www.bcnf.bc.ca/

5. "Neurofibromatosis." MediResource's Body and Health. N.p., n.d. Web. 03 May 2013.

## CHAPTER 5

1. "Brothers Dube Hit $106,000 - CTV News March 13." YouTube. YouTube, 17 Mar. 2011. Web. 02 Feb. 2013. <http://www.youtube.com/watch?v=qPMzxi1kjSc>.

2. "Help the Dube Brothers - 3 Kids Helping Kids." YouTube. YouTube, 20 Sept. 2012. Web. 02 Feb. 2013. <http://www.youtube.com/watch?v=52_-XgD07Pw>.

3. "Brothers Dube© - ONE - Official Song Video Now on ITunes." YouTube. YouTube, 23 June 2011. Web. 02 Feb. 2013. <http://www.youtube.com/watch?v=9YhEW9Egp6k>.

4. Netter, Sarah. "Haiti Earthquake Devastates Lives of Orphans, Unwanted Children." ABC News. ABC News Network, 14 Jan. 2010. Web. 03 May 2013.

## CHAPTER 6

1. Podmorow, Alaina. "The Troops Will Leave Afghanistan, But Our Duty Is Still On The Ground." The Globe and Mail. 23 Feb. 2011. Web. 02 Feb. 2013. <http://www.theglobeandmail.com/commentary/the-troops-will-leave-afghanistan-but-our-duty-is-still-on-the-ground/article567779/>.

2. http://www.theprovince.com/life/Kelowna+teen+feted+helping+girls+Afghanistan+education/7312966/story.html

3. Musick, Sueann. "Project Founder Tells Local Students Obstacles Facing Girl Students in Afghanistan." The News. 10 Oct. 2012. Web. 02 Feb. 2013. <http://www.ngnews.ca/News/Local/2012-10-10/article-3096731/Project-founder-tells-local-students-obstacles-facing-girl-students-in-Afghanistan/1>.

4. "School Enrollment." Canadian Women For Women In Afghanistan. N.p., n.d. Web. 03 May 2013.

## CHAPTER 7

1. Higson-Hughes, Kristin. "He Raised $10,000 To Save His Grandma's House!" Woman's World 7 May 2012: 44. Print.

2. "Noah's Dream Catcher Network." www.noahdreamnetwork.org. Web. 02 Feb. 2013. <http://www.noahdreamnetwork.org/index.php>.

3. http://noahsdreamcatchernetwork.wordpress.com/tag/noah-lamaide/

4. "On the Road: Noah's Dream Catcher Network." CBSNews. CBS Interactive, Web. 03 Feb. 2013. <http://www.cbsnews.com/video/watch/?id=7398327n>.

5. http://noahsdreamcatchernetwork.wordpress.com/tag/noah-lamaide/

6. Shupe, Jim. "NativeTech: A Three-Part FAQ on Dream Catchers." Native Tech. N.p., 26 July 1995. Web. 03 May 2013.

7. http://noahsdreamcatchernetwork.wordpress.com/tag/noah-lamaide/

8. Neubauer, Emily. "Local Teens Help Holiday Dreams Come True - WAOW - Newsline 9, Wausau News, Weather, Sports." Local Teens Help Holiday Dreams Come True - WAOW - Newsline 9, Wausau News, Weather, Sports. N.p., 05 Dec. 2012. Web. 03 Feb. 2013. <http://www.waow.com/story/20272170/2012/12/05/local-teens-help-holiday-dreams-come-true>.

9. "On the Road: Noah's Dream Catcher Network." CBSNews. CBS Interactive, Web. 03 Feb. 2013. <http://www.cbsnews.com/video/watch/?id=7398327n>.

10. "Noah's Dream Catcher Network." www.noahdreamnetwork.org. Web. 02 Feb. 2013. <http://www.noahdreamnetwork.org/index.php>.

## CHAPTER 8

1. 09 June 2013. <http://www.sophisticatesblackhairstyles.com/categorysbh-blogthis-girl-is-on-fire/>.

2. "Veteran Population." NATIONAL CENTER FOR VETERANS ANALYSIS AND STATISTICS. N.p., n.d. Web. 09 June 2013. <http://www.va.gov/vetdata/Veteran_Population.asp>.

3. "Interview With Glennita Williams." Girls For A Change. N.p., n.d. Web. 9 June 2013. <http://static.ow.ly/docs/Girls%20For%20A%20Change%20Interview%20with%20Glennita%20Williams_nGd.pdf>

4. "Cadet Programs." Civil Air Patrol - United States Air Force Auxiliary. N.p., n.d. Web. 09 June 2013. <http://www.gocivilairpatrol.com/about/civil_air_patrols_three_primary_missions/cadet-programs/>.

5. Wihbey, John. "U.S. Military Casualty Statistics and the Costs of War: Iraq, Afghanistan and Post-9/11 Conflicts." Journalists Resource RSS. N.p., 19 Feb. 2013. Web. 09 June 2013. <http://journalistsresource.org/studies/international/conflicts/us-military-casualty-statistics-costs-war-iraq-afghanistan-post-911>.

## CHAPTER 9

1. "2012 State Honoree Calista Pierce." YouTube. YouTube, 24 May 2012. Web. 03 Feb. 2013. <https://www.youtube.com/watch?v=u2D-gpsbOuk>.

2. "Make-A-Wish® Canada - Adopt-A-Wish Program." Make-A-Wish® Canada. N.p., n.d. Web. 03 May 2013.

3. Dallman, Kasey. "Calista Pierce, Amazing Young Wish Granter." Amazing Kids Magazine. Feb. 2012. Web. 3 Feb. 2013. <http://mag.amazing-kids.org/2012/01/31/amazing-kids-of-the-month-february-2012-calista-pierce/>.

## CHAPTER 10

1. WIFR." YouTube. YouTube, 01 Sept. 2009. Web. 03 Feb. 2013. <http://www.youtube.com/watch?v=4YRisyvUyxs>.

2. Yu, Hao, Dr., Lauren M. Wier, M.P.H., and Anne Elixhauser, Dr. "Hospital Stays For Children 2009: Statistical Brief #118." Agency for Healthcare Research and Quality. N.p., Aug. 2011. Web.

3. Hospital for Sick Children." Wikipedia. Wikimedia Foundation, 29 Apr. 2013. Web. 03 May 2013.

## CHAPTER 11

1. "Read Indeed: Join Maria's Effort to Collect One Million Books." Kare11.com. 15 July 2011. Web. 03 Feb. 2013. <http://www.kare11.com/news/extras/article/926707/26/Read-Indeed-Join-Marias-effort-to-collect-one-million-books>.

2. Read Indeed: Join Maria's Effort to Collect One Million Books." Kare11.com. 15 July 2011. Web. 03 Feb. 2013. <http://www.kare11.com/news/extras/article/926707/26/Read-Indeed-Join-Marias-effort-to-collect-one-million-books>.

3. "Read Indeed." Ivanhoe Medical Broadcast News. 03 Aug. 2011. Web. 03 Feb. 2013. <http://www.ivanhoe.com/channels/p_channelstory.cfm?storyid=27566>.

4. "Read Indeed." Ivanhoe Medical Broadcast News. 03 Aug. 2011. Web. 03 Feb. 2013. <http://www.ivanhoe.com/channels/p_channelstory.cfm?storyid=27566>.

5. "Maria Keller: Eleven Who Care Winner." Kare11.com. 15 July 2012. Web. 03 Feb. 2013. <http://www.kare11.com/community/11whocare/article/956973/402/Eleven-Who-Care-Winner-Maria-Keller>.

6. "First Book Statistics: Literacy in America." First Book. N.p., n.d. Web. 3 May 2013.

7. "First Book Statistics: Literacy in America." First Book. N.p., n.d. Web. 3 May 2013.

## CHAPTER 12

1. Jakobschuk, Laura. "Brothers Give The Gift Of Hockey To Other Kids Local." St. Catharines Standard. 14 Dec. 2011. Web. 03 Feb. 2013. <http://www.stcatharinesstandard.ca/2011/12/14/brothers-give-the-gift-of-hockey-to-other-kids>.

2. Mirtle, James. "Bauer Takes on Sagging Minor Hockey Enrolment." The Globe and Mail. N.p., 03 Oct. 2012. Web. 03 May 2013.

## CHAPTER 13

1. Grossman, Samantha. "China to Stop Giving Orphans Surnames Like 'State,' 'Party.'" Time News Feed. N.p., 14 Feb. 2012. Web. 03 May 2013.

## CHAPTER 14

1. "Pay It Forward Kids Drive By." YouTube. YouTube, 25 June 2012. Web. 03 Feb. 2013. <http://www.youtube.com/watch?v=0lX8B6_5-c4>.

2. Johnson, Charley. "Founder Bio." Pay It Forward Experience. N.p., n.d. Web. 03 May 2013.

3. Ryan Hyde, Catherine. "Pay It Forward." Catherine Ryan Hyde. N.p., n.d. Web. 03 May 2013.

# INDEX